MEDITERRANEAN DIET 2022

TASTY RECIPES EASY TO MAKE

GARY CAPRA

Table of Contents

Seafood Linguine 9

Ginger Shrimp & Tomato Relish 11

Shrimp & Pasta 14

Poached Cod 16

Mussels in White Wine 18

Dilly Salmon 20

Smooth Salmon 22

Tuna Melody 23

Sea Cheese 24

Healthy Steaks 25

Herbal Salmon 26

Smokey Glazed Tuna 27

Crusty Halibut 28

Fit Tuna 29

Hot and Fresh Fishy Steaks 30

Mussels O' Marine 31

Slow Cooker Mediterranean Beef Roast 32

Slow Cooker Mediterranean Beef with Artichokes 34

Skinny Slow Cooker Mediterranean Style Pot Roast 36

Slow Cooker Meatloaf 38

Slow Cooker Mediterranean Beef Hoagies 40

Mediterranean Pork Roast 42

Beef Pizza 44

Beef & Bulgur Meatballs 47

Tasty Beef and Broccoli 49

Beef Corn Chili 50

Balsamic Beef Dish 51

Soy Sauce Beef Roast 53

Rosemary Beef Chuck Roast 55

Pork Chops and Tomato Sauce 57

Chicken with Caper Sauce 58

Turkey Burgers with Mango Salsa 60

Herb-Roasted Turkey Breast 62

Chicken Sausage and Peppers 64

Chicken Piccata 66

One-Pan Tuscan Chicken 68

Chicken Kapama 70

Spinach and Feta–Stuffed Chicken Breasts 72

Rosemary Baked Chicken Drumsticks 74

Chicken with Onions, Potatoes, Figs, and Carrots 75

Chicken Gyros with Tzatziki 77

Moussaka 79

Dijon and Herb Pork Tenderloin 81

Steak with Red Wine–Mushroom Sauce 83

Greek Meatballs 86

Lamb with String Beans 88

Chicken in Tomato-Balsamic Pan Sauce 90

Brown Rice, Feta, Fresh Pea, and Mint Salad 92

Whole Grain Pita Bread Stuffed with Olives and Chickpeas 94

Roasted Carrots with Walnuts and Cannellini Beans 96

Seasoned Buttered Chicken 98

Double Cheesy Bacon Chicken 100

Shrimps with Lemon and Pepper 102

Breaded and Spiced Halibut 104

Curry Salmon with Mustard 106

Walnut-Rosemary Crusted Salmon 107

Quick Tomato Spaghetti 109

Chili Oregano Baked Cheese 111

311. Crispy Italian Chicken 111

Sea Bass in a Pocket 113

Creamy Smoked Salmon Pasta 115

Slow Cooker Greek Chicken 117

Chicken Gyros 119

Slow Cooker Chicken Cassoulet 121

Greek Style Turkey Roast 124

Garlic Chicken with Couscous 126

Chicken Karahi 128

Chicken Cacciatore with Orzo 130

Slow Cooked Daube Provencal 132

Osso Bucco 134

Slow Cooker Beef Bourguignon 136

Balsamic Beef 139

Veal Pot Roast 141

Mediterranean Rice and Sausage 143

Spanish Meatballs 144

Cauliflower Steaks with Olive Citrus Sauce 146

Pistachio Mint Pesto Pasta 148

Burst Cherry Tomato Sauce with Angel Hair Pasta 150

Baked Tofu with Sun-Dried Tomatoes and Artichokes 152

Baked Mediterranean Tempeh with Tomatoes and Garlic 154

Roasted Portobello Mushrooms with Kale and Red Onion 157

Ricotta, Basil, and Pistachio–Stuffed Zucchini 161

Farro with Roasted Tomatoes and Mushrooms 163

Baked Orzo with Eggplant, Swiss Chard, and Mozzarella...................... 166

Barley Risotto with Tomatoes.. 168

Chickpeas and Kale with Spicy Pomodoro Sauce................................. 170

Roasted Feta with Kale and Lemon Yogurt 172

Roasted Eggplant and Chickpeas with Tomato Sauce........................... 174

Baked Falafel Sliders 176

Portobello Caprese... 178

Mushroom and Cheese Stuffed Tomatoes... 180

Tabbouleh... 182

Spicy Broccoli Rabe And Artichoke Hearts 184

Shakshuka... 186

Spanakopita 188

Tagine... 190

Citrus Pistachios and Asparagus 192

Tomato and Parsley Stuffed Eggplant 194

Ratatouille 196

Gemista 198

Stuffed Cabbage Rolls 200

Brussels Sprouts with Balsamic Glaze 202

Spinach Salad with Citrus Vinaigrette 204

Simple Celery and Orange Salad 205

Fried Eggplant Rolls.. 207

Roasted Veggies and Brown Rice Bowl 209

Cauliflower Hash with Carrots 211

Garlicky Zucchini Cubes with Mint 212

Zucchini and Artichokes Bowl with Faro 213

5-Ingredient Zucchini Fritters 215

Seafood Linguine

Preparation Time : 10 minutes

Cooking Time : 35 minutes

Servings : 2

Difficulty Level : Difficult

Ingredients:

- 2 Cloves Garlic, Chopped
- 4 Ounces Linguine, Whole Wheat
- 1 Tablespoon Olive Oil
- 14 Ounces Tomatoes, Canned & Diced
- 1/2 Tablespoon Shallot, Chopped
- 1/4 Cup White Wine
- Sea Salt & Black Pepper to Taste
- 6 Cherrystone Clams, Cleaned
- 4 Ounces Tilapia, Sliced into 1 Inch Strips
- 4 Ounces Dry Sea Scallops
- 1/8 Cup Parmesan Cheese, Grated
- 1/2 Teaspoon Marjoram, Chopped & Fresh

Directions:

Boil the water in pot, then cook pasta until tender which should take roughly eight minutes. Drain and then rinse your pasta.

Heat your oil using a large skillet over medium heat, and then once your oil is hot stir in your garlic and shallot. Cook for a minute, and stir often.

Increase the heat to medium-high before adding your salt, wine, pepper and tomatoes, bringing it to a simmer. Cook for one minute more.

Add your clams next, covering and cooking for another two minutes.

Stir in your marjoram, scallops and fish next. Continue cooking until the fish is cook all the way through and your clams have opened up this will take up to five minutes, and get rid of any clams that do not open.

Spoon the sauce and your clams over the pasta, sprinkling with parmesan and marjoram before serving. Serve warm.

Nutrition (for 100g): 329 calories 12g fats 10g carbohydrates 33g protein 836mg sodium

Ginger Shrimp & Tomato Relish

Preparation Time : 10 minutes

Cooking Time : 15 minutes

Servings : 2

Difficulty Level : Difficult

Ingredients:

- 1 1/2 Tablespoons Vegetable Oil
- 1 Clove Garlic, Minced
- 10 Shrimp, Extra Large, Peeled & Tails Left On
- 3/4 Tablespoons Finger, Grated & Peeled
- 1 Green Tomatoes, Halved
- 2 Plum Tomatoes, Halved
- 1 Tablespoon Lime Juice, Fresh
- 1/2 Teaspoon Sugar
- 1/2 Tablespoon Jalapeno with Seeds, Fresh & Minced
- 1/2 Tablespoon Basil, Fresh & Chopped
- 1/2 Tablespoons Cilantro, Chopped & Fresh
- 10 Skewers
- Sea Salt & Black Pepper to Taste

Directions:

Immerse your skewers in a pan of water for at least a half hour.

Stir your garlic and ginger together in a bowl, transferring half to a larger bowl and stirring it with two tablespoons of your oil. Add in the shrimp, and make sure they are well coated.

Cover and transfer it in the fridge for at least a half hour, and then allow it to refrigerate.

Heat your grill to high, and grease the grates lightly using oil. Get out a bowl and toss your plum and green tomatoes with the remaining tablespoon of oil, seasoning with salt and pepper.

Grill your tomatoes with the cut side up and the skins should be charred. The flesh of your tomato should be tender, which will take about four to six minutes for the plum tomato and about ten minutes for the green tomato.

Remove the skins once the tomatoes are cool enough to handle, and then discard the seeds. Chop the tomatoes flesh fine, adding it to the reserved ginger and garlic. Add in your sugar, jalapeno, lime juice and basil.

Season your shrimp using salt and pepper threading them onto the skewers, and then grill until they turn opaque, which is about two minutes on each side. Place the shrimp on a platter with your relish and enjoy.

Nutrition (for 100g): 391 calories 13g fats 11g carbohydrates 34g protein 693mg sodium

Shrimp & Pasta

Preparation Time : 10 minutes

Cooking Time : 10 minutes

Servings : 2

Difficulty Level : Average

Ingredients:

- 2 Cups Angel Hair Pasta, Cooked
- 1/2 lb. Medium Shrimp, Peeled
- 1 Clove Garlic, Minced
- 1 Cup Tomato, Chopped
- 1 Teaspoon Olive Oil
- 1/6 Cup Kalamata Olives, Pitted & Chopped
- 1/8 Cup Basil, Fresh & Sliced Thin
- 1 Tablespoon Capers, Drained
- 1/8 Cup Feta Cheese, Crumbled
- Dash Black Pepper

Directions:

Cook your pasta per package instructions, and then heat your olive oil in a skillet using medium-high heat. Cook your garlic for half a minute, and then add your shrimp. Sauté for a minute more.

Add your basil and tomato, and then reduce the heat to allow it to simmer for three minutes. Your tomato should be tender.

Stir in your olives and capers. Add a dash of black pepper, and combine your shrimp mix and pasta to serve. Top with cheese before serving warm.

Nutrition (for 100g): 357 calories 11g fats 9g carbohydrates 30g protein 871mg sodium

Poached Cod

Preparation Time : 10 minutes

Cooking Time : 25 minutes

Servings : 2

Difficulty Level : Average

Ingredients:

- 2 Cod Filets, 6 Ounces
- Sea Salt & Black Pepper to Taste
- 1/4 Cup Dry White Wine
- 1/4 Cup Seafood Stock
- 2 Cloves Garlic, Minced
- 1 Bay Leaf
- 1/2 Teaspoon Sage, Fresh & Chopped
- 2 Rosemary Sprigs to Garnish

Directions:

Start by turning your oven to 375, and then season the fillets with salt and pepper. Place them in a baking pan, and add in your stock, garlic, wine, sage and bay leaf. Cover well, and then bake for twenty minutes. Your fish should be flaky when tested with a fork.

Use a spatula to remove each fillet, placing the liquid over high heat and cooking to reduce in half. This should take ten minutes, and you need to stir frequently. Serve dripped in poaching liquid and garnished with a rosemary sprig.

Nutrition (for 100g): 361 calories 10g fats 9g carbohydrates 34g protein 783mg sodium

Mussels in White Wine

Preparation Time : 5 minutes

Cooking Time : 10 minutes

Servings : 2

Difficulty Level : Difficult

Ingredients:

- 2 lbs. Live Mussels, Fresh
- 1 Cup Dry White Wine
- 1/4 Teaspoon Sea Salt, Fine
- 3 Cloves Garlic, Minced
- 2 Teaspoons Shallots, Diced
- 1/4 Cup Parsley, Fresh & Chopped, Divided
- 2 Tablespoons olive Oil
- 1/4 Lemon, Juiced

Directions:

Get out a colander and scrub your mussels, rinsing them using cold water. Discard mussels that will not close if they're tapped, and then use a paring knife to remove the beard from each one.

Get out stockpot, placing it over medium-high heat, and add in your garlic, shallots, wine and parsley. Bring it to a simmer. Once it's at a steady simmer, add in your mussels and cover. Allow them to simmer for five to seven minutes. Make sure they do not overcook.

Use a slotted spoon to remove them, and add your lemon juice and olive oil into the pot. Stir well, and pour the broth over your mussels before serving with parsley.

Nutrition (for 100g): 345 calories 9g fats 18g carbohydrates 37g protein 693mg sodium

Dilly Salmon

Preparation Time : 10 minutes

Cooking Time : 15 minutes

Servings : 2

Difficulty Level : Average

Ingredients:

- 2 Salmon Fillets, 6 Ounces Each
- 1 Tablespoon Olive Oil
- 1/2 Tangerine, Juiced
- 2 Teaspoons Orange Zest
- 2 Tablespoons Dill, Fresh & Chopped
- Sea Salt & Black Pepper to Taste

Directions:

Prepare oven to 375 degrees, and then get out two ten-inch pieces of foil. Rub your filets down with olive oil on both side before seasoning with salt and pepper, placing each fillet into a piece of foil.

Drizzle your orange juice over each one, and then top with orange zest and dill. Fold your packet closed, making sure it has two inches of air space within the foil so your fish can steam, and then place them on a baking dish.

Bake for fifteen minutes before opening the packets, and transfer to two serving plates. Pour the sauce over the top of each before serving.

Nutrition (for 100g): 366 calories 14g fats 9g carbohydrates 36g protein 689mg sodium

Smooth Salmon

Preparation Time : 8 minutes

Cooking Time : 8 minutes

Servings : 2

Difficulty Level : Easy

Ingredients:

- Salmon, 6-ounce fillet
- Lemon, 2 slices
- Capers, 1 tablespoon
- Sea salt and pepper, 1/8 teaspoon
- Extra virgin olive oil, 1 tablespoon

Directions:

Place a clean skillet over a medium heat to prepare for 3 minutes. Place olive oil on a plate, and coat the salmon completely. Cook the salmon over a high heat in the skillet.

Top the salmon with the rest of the ingredients, and turn to cook each side. Notice when both sides are brown. It may take 3-5 minutes each side. Make sure the salmon is cooked by testing with a fork.

Serve with lemon slices.

Nutrition (for 100g): 371 Calories 25.1g Fat 0.9g Carbohydrates 33.7g Protein 782mg Sodium

Tuna Melody

Preparation Time : 20 minutes

Cooking Time : 20 minutes

Servings : 2

Difficulty Level : Easy

Ingredients:

- Tuna, 12 ounces
- Green onions, 1 for garnish
- Bell pepper, ¼, chopped
- Vinegar, 1 dash
- Salt and pepper to taste
- Avocados, 1, halved and pitted
- Greek yogurt, 2 tablespoons

Directions:

Mix the tuna with the vinegar, onion, yogurt, avocado and pepper in a bowl.

Add the seasonings, mix, and serve with the green onion garnish.

Nutrition (for 100g): 294 Calories 19g Fat 10g Carbohydrates 12g Protein 836mg Sodium

Sea Cheese

Preparation Time : 12 minutes

Cooking Time : 25 minutes

Servings : 2

Difficulty Level : Easy

Ingredients:

- Salmon, 6-ounce fillet
- Dried basil, 1 tablespoon
- Cheese, 2 tablespoons, grated
- Tomato, 1, sliced
- Extra virgin olive oil, 1 tablespoon

Directions:

Prepare a baking oven at 375 F. Layer aluminum foil in a baking dish, and spray with cooking oil. Carefully transfer the salmon to the baking tray and top with the rest of the ingredients.

Let the salmon brown for 20 minutes. Allow to cool for five minutes, and transfer to a serving plate. You will see the topping in the middle of the salmon.

Nutrition (for 100g): 411 Calories 26.6g Fat 1.6g Carbohydrates 8g Protein 822mg Sodium

Healthy Steaks

Preparation Time : 10 minutes

Cooking Time : 20 minutes

Servings : 2

Difficulty Level : Easy

Ingredients:

- Olive oil, 1 teaspoon
- Halibut steak, 8 ounces
- Garlic, ½ teaspoon, minced
- Butter, 1 tablespoon
- Salt and pepper to taste

Directions:

Heat a skillet and add the oil. Over a medium flame, brown the steaks in a pan, melt the butter with the garlic, salt and pepper. Add the steaks, toss to coat, and serve.

Nutrition (for 100g): 284 Calories 17g Fat 0.2g Carbohydrates 8g Protein 755mg Sodium

Herbal Salmon

Preparation Time : 8 minutes

Cooking Time : 18 minutes

Servings : 2

Difficulty Level : Easy

Ingredients:

- Salmon, 2 fillets without skin
- Coarse salt to taste
- Extra virgin olive oil, 1 tablespoon
- Lemon, 1, sliced
- Fresh rosemary, 4 sprigs

Directions:

Preheat the oven to 400F. Situate aluminum foil in a baking dish, and place salmon on top. Top the salmon with the rest of the ingredients and bake for 20 minutes. Serve immediately with lemon slices.

Nutrition (for 100g): 257 Calories 18g Fat 2.7g Carbohydrates 7g Protein 836mg Sodium

Smokey Glazed Tuna

Preparation Time : 35 minutes

Cooking Time : 10 minutes

Servings : 2

Difficulty Level : Easy

Ingredients:

- Tuna, 4-ounce steaks

- Orange juice, 1 tablespoon

- Minced garlic, ½ clove

- Lemon juice, ½ teaspoon

- Fresh parsley, 1 tablespoon, chopped

- Soy sauce, 1 tablespoon

- Extra virgin olive oil, 1 tablespoon

- Ground black pepper, ¼ teaspoon

- Oregano, ¼ teaspoon

Directions:

Pick a mixing dish, and add all the ingredients, except the tuna. Mix well, and then add the tuna to marinade. Refrigerate this mixture for half an hour. Heat a grill pan and cook the tuna on each side for 5 minutes. Serve when cooked.

Nutrition (for 100g): 200 Calories 7.9g Fat 0.3g Carbohydrates 10g Protein 734mg Sodium

Crusty Halibut

Preparation Time : 20 minutes

Cooking Time : 15 minutes

Servings : 2

Difficulty Level : Easy

Ingredients:

- Parsley to top
- Fresh dill, 2 tablespoons, chopped
- Fresh chives, 2 tablespoons, chopped
- Olive oil, 1 tablespoon
- Salt and pepper to taste
- Halibut, fillets, 6 ounces
- Lemon zest, ½ teaspoon, finely grated
- Greek yogurt, 2 tablespoons

Directions:

Preheat the oven to 400F. Line a baking sheet with foil. Add all the ingredients to a wide dish, and marinate the fillets. Rinse and dry the fillets; then add to the oven and bake for 15 minutes.

Nutrition (for 100g): 273 Calories 7.2g Fat 0.4g Carbohydrates 9g Protein 783mg Sodium

Fit Tuna

Preparation Time : 15 minutes

Cooking Time : 10 minutes

Servings : 2

Difficulty Level : Easy

Ingredients:

- Egg, ½
- Onion, 1 tablespoon, finely chopped
- Celery to top
- Salt and pepper to taste
- Garlic, 1 clove, minced
- Canned tuna, 7 ounces
- Greek yogurt, 2 tablespoons

Directions:

Drain the tuna, and add the egg and yogurt with the garlic, salt and pepper.

In a bowl, combine this mixture with onions and shape into patties. Take a large skillet and brown the patties for 3 minutes per side. Drain and serve.

Nutrition (for 100g): 230 Calories 13g Fat 0.8g Carbohydrates 10g Protein 866mg Sodium

Hot and Fresh Fishy Steaks

Preparation Time : 14 minutes

Cooking Time : 14 minutes

Servings : 2

Difficulty Level : Easy

Ingredients:

- Garlic, 1 clove, minced
- Lemon juice, 1 tablespoon
- Brown sugar, 1 tablespoon
- Halibut steak, 1 pound
- Salt and pepper to taste
- Soy sauce, ¼ teaspoon
- Butter, 1 teaspoon
- Greek yogurt, 2 tablespoons

Directions:

Over a medium flame, preheat the grill. Mix the butter, sugar, yogurt, lemon juice, soy sauce and seasonings in a bowl. Warm the mixture in a pan. Use this mixture to brush onto the steak while cooking on the griller. Serve hot.

Nutrition (for 100g): 412 Calories 19.4g Fat 7.6g Carbohydrates 11g Protein 788mg Sodium

Mussels O' Marine

Preparation Time : 20 minutes

Cooking Time : 10 minutes

Servings : 2

Difficulty Level : Easy

Ingredients:

- Mussels, scrubbed and debearded, 1 pound
- Coconut milk, ½ cup
- Cayenne pepper, 1 teaspoon
- Fresh lemon juice, 1 tablespoon
- Garlic, 1 teaspoon, minced
- Cilantro, freshly chopped for topping
- Brown sugar, 1 teaspoon

Directions:

Mix all the ingredients, except the mussels in a pot. Heat the mixture and bring it to the boil. Add the mussels, and cook for 10 minutes. Serve in a dish with the boiled liquid.

Nutrition (for 100g): 483 Calories 24.4g Fat 21.6g Carbohydrates 1.2g Protein 499mg Sodium

Slow Cooker Mediterranean Beef Roast

Preparation Time : 10 minutes

Cooking Time : 10 hours and 10 minutes

Servings : 6

Difficulty Level : Average

Ingredients:

- 3 pounds Chuck roast, boneless
- 2 teaspoons Rosemary
- ½ cup Tomatoes, sun-dried and chopped
- 10 cloves Grated garlic
- ½ cup Beef stock
- 2 tablespoons Balsamic vinegar
- ¼ cup Chopped Italian parsley, fresh
- ¼ cup Chopped olives
- 1 teaspoon Lemon zest
- ¼ cup Cheese grits

Directions:

In the slow cooker, put garlic, sun dried tomatoes, and the beef roast. Add beef stock and Rosemary. Close the cooker and slow cook for 10 hours.

After cooking is over, remove the beef, and shred the meet. Discard the fat. Add back the shredded meat to the slow cooker and simmer for 10 minutes. In a small bowl combine lemon zest, parsley, and olives. Cool the mixture until you are ready to serve. Garnish using the refrigerated mix.

Serve it over pasta or egg noodles. Top it with cheese grits.

Nutrition (for 100g): 314 Calories 19g Fat 1g Carbohydrate 32g Protein 778mg Sodium

Slow Cooker Mediterranean Beef with Artichokes

Preparation Time : 3 hours and 20 minutes

Cooking Time : 7 hours and 8 minutes

Servings : 6

Difficulty Level : Easy

Ingredients:

- 2 pounds Beef for stew
- 14 ounces Artichoke hearts
- 1 tablespoon Grape seed oil
- 1 Diced onion
- 32 ounces Beef broth
- 4 cloves Garlic, grated
- 14½ ounces Tinned tomatoes, diced
- 15 ounces Tomato sauce
- 1 teaspoon Dried oregano
- ½ cup Pitted, chopped olives
- 1 teaspoon Dried parsley
- 1 teaspoon Dried oregano
- ½ teaspoon Ground cumin
- 1 teaspoon Dried basil
- 1 Bay leaf
- ½ teaspoon Salt

Directions:

In a large non-stick skillet pour some oil and bring to medium-high heat. Roast the beef until it turns brown on both the sides. Transfer the beef into a slow cooker.

Add in beef broth, diced tomatoes, tomato sauce, salt and combine. Pour in beef broth, diced tomatoes, oregano, olives, basil, parsley, bay leaf, and cumin. Combine the mixture thoroughly.

Close and cook on low heat for 7 hours. Discard the bay leaf at the time serving. Serve hot.

Nutrition (for 100g): 416 Calories 5g Fat 14.1g Carbohydrates 29.9g Protein 811mg Sodium

Skinny Slow Cooker Mediterranean Style Pot Roast

Preparation Time : 30 minutes

Cooking Time : 8 hours

Servings : 10

Difficulty Level : Difficult

Ingredients:

- 4 pounds Eye of round roast
- 4 cloves Garlic
- 2 teaspoons Olive oil
- 1 teaspoon Freshly ground black pepper
- 1 cup Chopped onions
- 4 Carrots, chopped
- 2 teaspoons Dried Rosemary
- 2 Chopped celery stalks
- 28 ounces Crushed tomatoes in the can
- 1 cup Low sodium beef broth
- 1 cup Red wine
- 2 teaspoons Salt

Directions:

Season the beef roast with salt, garlic, and pepper and set aside. Pour oil in a non-stick skillet and bring to medium-high heat. Put the beef into it and roast until it becomes brown on all sides. Now, transfer the roasted beef into a 6-quart slow cooker. Add carrots, onion, rosemary, and celery into the skillet. Continue cooking until the onion and vegetable become soft.

Stir in the tomatoes and wine into this vegetable mixture. Add beef broth and tomato mixture into the slow cooker along with the vegetable mixture. Close and cook on low for 8 hours.

Once the meat gets cooked, remove it from the slow cooker and place it on a cutting board and wrap with an aluminum foil. To thicken the sauce, then transfer it into a saucepan and boil it under low heat until it reaches to the required consistency. Discard fats before serving.

Nutrition (for 100g): 260 Calories 6g Fat 8.7g Carbohydrates 37.6g Protein 588mg Sodium

Slow Cooker Meatloaf

Preparation Time : 10 minutes

Cooking Time : 6 hours and 10 minutes

Servings : 8

Difficulty Level : Average

Ingredients:

- 2 pounds Ground bison
- 1 Grated zucchini
- 2 large Eggs
- Olive oil cooking spray as required
- 1 Zucchini, shredded
- ½ cup Parsley, fresh, finely chopped
- ½ cup Parmesan cheese, shredded
- 3 tablespoons Balsamic vinegar
- 4 Garlic cloves, grated
- 2 tablespoons Onion minced
- 1 tablespoon Dried oregano
- ½ teaspoon Ground black pepper
- ½ teaspoon Kosher salt
- For the topping:
- ¼ cup Shredded Mozzarella cheese
- ¼ cup Ketchup without sugar
- ¼ cup Freshly chopped parsley

Directions:

Stripe line the inside of a six-quart slow cooker with aluminum foil. Spray non-stick cooking oil over it.

In a large bowl combine ground bison or extra lean ground sirloin, zucchini, eggs, parsley, balsamic vinegar, garlic, dried oregano, sea or kosher salt, minced dry onion, and ground black pepper.

Situate this mixture into the slow cooker and form an oblong shaped loaf. Cover the cooker, set on a low heat and cook for 6 hours. After cooking, open the cooker and spread ketchup all over the meatloaf.

Now, place the cheese above the ketchup as a new layer and close the slow cooker. Let the meatloaf sit on these two layers for about 10 minutes or until the cheese starts to melt. Garnish with fresh parsley, and shredded Mozzarella cheese.

Nutrition (for 100g): 320 Calories 2g Fat 4g Carbohydrates 26g Protein 681mg Sodium

Slow Cooker Mediterranean Beef Hoagies

Preparation Time : 10 minutes

Cooking Time : 13 hours

Servings : 6

Difficulty Level : Average

Ingredients:

- 3 pounds Beef top round roast fatless
- ½ teaspoon Onion powder
- ½ teaspoon Black pepper
- 3 cups Low sodium beef broth
- 4 teaspoons Salad dressing mix
- 1 Bay leaf
- 1 tablespoon Garlic, minced
- 2 Red bell peppers, thin strips cut
- 16 ounces Pepperoncino
- 8 slices Sargento Provolone, thin
- 2 ounces Gluten-free bread
- ½ teaspoon salt
- For seasoning:
- 1½ tablespoon Onion powder
- 1½ tablespoon Garlic powder
- 2 tablespoon Dried parsley
- 1 tablespoon stevia
- ½ teaspoon Dried thyme

- 1 tablespoon Dried oregano

- 2 tablespoons Black pepper

- 1 tablespoon Salt

- 6 Cheese slices

Directions:

Dry the roast with a paper towel. Combine black pepper, onion powder and salt in a small bowl and rub the mixture over the roast. Place the seasoned roast into a slow cooker.

Add broth, salad dressing mix, bay leaf, and garlic to the slow cooker. Combine it gently. Close and set to low cooking for 12 hours. After cooking, remove the bay leaf.

Take out the cooked beef and shred the beef meet. Put back the shredded beef and add bell peppers and. Add bell peppers and pepperoncino into the slow cooker. Cover the cooker and low cook for 1 hour. Before serving, top each of the bread with 3 ounces of the meat mixture. Top it with a cheese slice. The liquid gravy can be used as a dip.

Nutrition (for 100g): 442 Calories 11.5g Fat 37g Carbohydrates 49g Protein 735mg Sodium

Mediterranean Pork Roast

Preparation Time : 10 minutes

Cooking Time : 8 hours and 10 minutes

Servings : 6

Difficulty Level : Average

Ingredients:

- 2 tablespoons Olive oil
- 2 pounds Pork roast
- ½ teaspoon Paprika
- ¾ cup Chicken broth
- 2 teaspoons Dried sage
- ½ tablespoon Garlic minced
- ¼ teaspoon Dried marjoram
- ¼ teaspoon Dried Rosemary
- 1 teaspoon Oregano
- ¼ teaspoon Dried thyme
- 1 teaspoon Basil
- ¼ teaspoon Kosher salt

Directions:

In a small bowl mix broth, oil, salt, and spices. In a skillet pour olive oil and bring to medium-high heat. Put the pork into it and roast until all sides become brown.

Take out the pork after cooking and poke the roast all over with a knife. Place the poked pork roast into a 6-quart crock pot. Now, pour the small bowl mixture liquid all over the roast.

Seal crock pot and cook on low for 8 hours. After cooking, remove it from the crock pot on to a cutting board and shred into pieces. Afterward, add the shredded pork back into the crockpot. Simmer it another 10 minutes. Serve along with feta cheese, pita bread, and tomatoes.

Nutrition (for 100g): 361 Calories 10.4g Fat 0.7g Carbohydrates 43.8g Protein 980mg Sodium

Beef Pizza

Preparation Time : 20 minutes

Cooking Time : 50 minutes

Servings : 10

Difficulty Level : Difficult

Ingredients:

- <u>For Crust:</u>
- 3 cups all-purpose flour
- 1 tablespoon sugar
- 2¼ teaspoons active dry yeast
- 1 teaspoon salt
- 2 tablespoons olive oil
- 1 cup warm water
- <u>For Topping:</u>
- 1-pound ground beef
- 1 medium onion, chopped
- 2 tablespoons tomato paste
- 1 tablespoon ground cumin
- Salt and ground black pepper, as required
- ¼ cup water
- 1 cup fresh spinach, chopped
- 8 ounces artichoke hearts, quartered
- 4 ounces fresh mushrooms, sliced

- 2 tomatoes, chopped

- 4 ounces feta cheese, crumbled

Directions:

For crust:

Mix the flour, sugar, yeast and salt with a stand mixer, using the dough hook. Add 2 tablespoons of the oil and warm water and knead until a smooth and elastic dough is formed.

Make a ball of the dough and set aside for about 15 minutes.

Situate the dough onto a lightly floured surface and roll into a circle. Situate the dough into a lightly, greased round pizza pan and gently, press to fit. Set aside for about 10-15 minutes. Coat the crust with some oil. Preheat the oven to 400 degrees F.

For topping:

Fry beef in a nonstick skillet over medium-high heat for about 4-5 minutes. Mix in the onion and cook for about 5 minutes, stirring frequently. Add the tomato paste, cumin, salt, black pepper and water and stir to combine.

Set the heat to medium and cook for about 5-10 minutes. Remove from the heat and set aside. Place the beef mixture over the pizza crust and top with the spinach, followed by the artichokes, mushrooms, tomatoes, and Feta cheese.

Bake until the cheese is melted. Remove from the oven and set aside for about 3-5 minutes before slicing. Cut into desired sized slices and serve.

Nutrition (for 100g): 309 Calories 8.7g Fat 3.7g Carbohydrates 3.3g Protein 732mg Sodium

Beef & Bulgur Meatballs

Preparation Time : 20 minutes

Cooking Time : 28 minutes

Servings : 6

Difficulty Level : Average

Ingredients:

- ¾ cup uncooked bulgur
- 1-pound ground beef
- ¼ cup shallots, minced
- ¼ cup fresh parsley, minced
- ½ teaspoon ground allspice
- ½ teaspoon ground cumin
- ½ teaspoon ground cinnamon
- ¼ teaspoon red pepper flakes, crushed
- Salt, as required
- 1 tablespoon olive oil

Directions:

In a large bowl of the cold water, soak the bulgur for about 30 minutes. Drain the bulgur well and then, squeeze with your hands to remove the excess water. In a food processor, add the bulgur, beef, shallot, parsley, spices, salt, and pulse until a smooth mixture is formed.

Situate the mixture into a bowl and refrigerate, covered for about 30 minutes. Remove from the refrigerator and make equal sized balls from the beef mixture. In a large nonstick skillet, heat the oil over medium-high heat and cook the meatballs in 2 batches for about 13-14 minutes, flipping frequently. Serve warm.

Nutrition (for 100g): 228 Calories 7.4g Fat 0.1g Carbohydrates 3.5g Protein 766mg Sodium

Tasty Beef and Broccoli

Preparation Time : 10 minutes

Cooking Time : 15 minutes

Servings : 4

Difficulty Level : Easy

Ingredients:

- 1 and ½ lbs. flanks steak
- 1 tbsp. olive oil
- 1 tbsp. tamari sauce
- 1 cup beef stock
- 1-pound broccoli, florets separated

Directions:

Combine steak strips with oil and tamari, toss and set aside for 10 minutes. Select your instant pot on sauté mode, place beef strips and brown them for 4 minutes on each side. Stir in stock, cover the pot again and cook on high for 8 minutes. Stir in broccoli, cover and cook on high for 4 minutes more. Portion everything between plates and serve. Enjoy!

Nutrition (for 100g): 312 Calories 5g Fat 20g Carbohydrates 4g Protein 694mg Sodium

Beef Corn Chili

Preparation Time : 8-10 minutes

Cooking Time : 30 minutes

Servings : 8

Difficulty Level : Average

Ingredients:

- 2 small onions, chopped (finely)
- ¼ cup canned corn
- 1 tablespoon oil
- 10 ounces lean ground beef
- 2 small chili peppers, diced

Directions:

Turn on the instant pot. Click "SAUTE". Pour the oil then stir in the onions, chili pepper, and beef; cook until turn translucent and softened. Pour the 3 cups water in the Cooking pot; mix well.

Seal the lid. Select "MEAT/STEW". Adjust the timer to 20 minutes. Allow to cook until the timer turns to zero.

Click "CANCEL" then "NPR" for natural release pressure for about 8-10 minutes. Open then place the dish in serving plates. Serve.

Nutrition (for 100g): 94 Calories 5g Fat 2g Carbohydrates 7g Protein 477mg Sodium

Balsamic Beef Dish

Preparation Time : 5 minutes

Cooking Time : 55 minutes

Servings : 8

Difficulty Level : Average

Ingredients:

- 3 pounds chuck roast
- 3 cloves garlic, thinly sliced
- 1 tablespoon oil
- 1 teaspoon flavored vinegar
- ½ teaspoon pepper
- ½ teaspoon rosemary
- 1 tablespoon butter
- ½ teaspoon thyme
- ¼ cup balsamic vinegar
- 1 cup beef broth

Directions:

Slice the slits in the roast and stuff in garlic slices all over. Combine flavored vinegar, rosemary, pepper, thyme and rub the mixture over the roast. Select the pot on sauté mode and mix in oil, allow the oil to heat up. Cook both side of the roast.

Take it out and set aside. Stir in butter, broth, balsamic vinegar and deglaze the pot. Return the roast and close the lid, then cook on HIGH pressure for 40 minutes.

Perform a quick release. Serve!

Nutrition (for 100g): 393 Calories 15g Fat 25g Carbohydrates 37g Protein 870mg Sodium

Soy Sauce Beef Roast

Preparation Time : 8 minutes

Cooking Time : 35 minutes

Servings : 2-3

Difficulty Level : Average

Ingredients:

- ½ teaspoon beef bouillon
- 1 ½ teaspoon rosemary
- ½ teaspoon minced garlic
- 2 pounds roast beef
- 1/3 cup soy sauce

Directions:

Combine the soy sauce, bouillon, rosemary, and garlic together in a mixing bowl.

Turn on your instant pot. Place the roast, and pour enough water to cover the roast; gently stir to mix well. Seal it tight.

Click "MEAT/STEW" Cooking function; set pressure level to "HIGH" and set the Cooking time to 35 minutes. Let the pressure to build to cook the ingredients. Once done, click "CANCEL" setting then click "NPR" Cooking function to release the pressure naturally.

Gradually open the lid, and shred the meat. Mix in the shredded meat back in the potting mix and stir well. Transfer in serving containers. Serve warm.

Nutrition (for 100g): 423 Calories 14g Fat 12g Carbohydrates 21g Protein 884mg Sodium

Rosemary Beef Chuck Roast

Preparation Time : 5 minutes

Cooking Time : 45 minutes

Servings : 5-6

Difficulty Level : Average

Ingredients:

- 3 pounds chuck beef roast
- 3 garlic cloves
- ¼ cup balsamic vinegar
- 1 sprig fresh rosemary
- 1 sprig fresh thyme
- 1 cup of water
- 1 tablespoon vegetable oil
- Salt and pepper to taste

Directions:

Chop slices in the beef roast and place the garlic cloves in them. Rub the roast with the herbs, black pepper, and salt. Preheat your instant pot using the sauté setting and pour the oil. When warmed, mix in the beef roast and stir-cook until browned on all sides. Add the remaining ingredients; stir gently.

Seal tight and cook on high for 40 minutes using manual setting. Allow the pressure release naturally, about 10 minutes. Uncover and put the beef roast the serving plates, slice and serve.

Nutrition (for 100g): 542 Calories 11.2g Fat 8.7g Carbohydrates 55.2g Protein 710mg Sodium

Pork Chops and Tomato Sauce

Preparation Time : 10 minutes

Cooking Time : 20 minutes

Servings : 4

Difficulty Level : Easy

Ingredients:

- 4 pork chops, boneless
- 1 tablespoon soy sauce
- ¼ teaspoon sesame oil
- 1 and ½ cups tomato paste
- 1 yellow onion
- 8 mushrooms, sliced

Directions:

In a bowl, mix pork chops with soy sauce and sesame oil, toss and leave aside for 10 minutes. Set your instant pot on sauté mode, add pork chops and brown them for 5 minutes on each side. Stir in onion, and cook for 1-2 minutes more. Add tomato paste and mushrooms, toss, cover and cook on high for 8-9 minutes. Divide everything between plates and serve. Enjoy!

Nutrition (for 100g): 300 Calories 7g Fat 18g Carbohydrates 4g Protein 801mg Sodium

Chicken with Caper Sauce

Preparation Time : 10 minutes

Cooking Time : 18 minutes

Servings : 5

Difficulty Level : Difficult

Ingredients:

- <u>For Chicken:</u>
- 2 eggs
- Salt and ground black pepper, as required
- 1 cup dry breadcrumbs
- 2 tablespoons olive oil
- 1½ pounds skinless, boneless chicken breast halves, pounded into ¾inch thickness and cut into pieces
- <u>For Capers Sauce:</u>
- 3 tablespoons capers
- ½ cup dry white wine
- 3 tablespoons fresh lemon juice
- Salt and ground black pepper, as required
- 2 tablespoons fresh parsley, chopped

Directions:

For chicken: in a shallow dish, add the eggs, salt and black pepper and beat until well combined. In another shallow dish, place breadcrumbs. Soak the chicken pieces in egg mixture then coat with the breadcrumbs evenly. Shake off the excess breadcrumbs.

Cook the oil over medium heat and cook the chicken pieces for about 5-7 minutes per side or until desired doneness. With a slotted spoon, situate the chicken pieces onto a paper towel lined plate. With a piece of the foil, cover the chicken pieces to keep them warm.

In the same skillet, incorporate all the sauce ingredients except parsley and cook for about 2-3 minutes, stirring continuously. Mix in the parsley and remove from heat. Serve the chicken pieces with the topping of capers sauce.

Nutrition (for 100g): 352 Calories 13.5g Fat 1.9g Carbohydrates 1.2g Protein 741mg Sodium

Turkey Burgers with Mango Salsa

Preparation Time : 15 minutes

Cooking Time : 10 minutes

Servings : 6

Difficulty Level : Easy

Ingredients:

- 1½ pounds ground turkey breast
- 1 teaspoon sea salt, divided
- ¼ teaspoon freshly ground black pepper
- 2 tablespoons extra-virgin olive oil
- 2 mangos, peeled, pitted, and cubed
- ½ red onion, finely chopped
- Juice of 1 lime
- 1 garlic clove, minced
- ½ jalapeño pepper, seeded and finely minced
- 2 tablespoons chopped fresh cilantro leaves

Directions:

Form the turkey breast into 4 patties and season with ½ teaspoon of sea salt and the pepper. Cook the olive oil in a nonstick skillet until it shimmers. Add the turkey patties and cook for about 5 minutes per side until browned. While the patties cook, mix the mango, red onion, lime juice, garlic, jalapeño, cilantro, and remaining ½ teaspoon of sea salt in a small bowl. Spoon the salsa over the turkey patties and serve.

Nutrition (for 100g): 384 Calories 3g Fat 27g Carbohydrates 34g Protein 692mg Sodium

Herb-Roasted Turkey Breast

Preparation Time : 15 minutes

Cooking Time : 1½ hours (plus 20 minutes to rest)

Servings : 6

Difficulty Level : Average

Ingredients:

- 2 tablespoons extra-virgin olive oil
- 4 garlic cloves, minced
- Zest of 1 lemon
- 1 tablespoon chopped fresh thyme leaves
- 1 tablespoon chopped fresh rosemary leaves
- 2 tablespoons chopped fresh Italian parsley leaves
- 1 teaspoon ground mustard
- 1 teaspoon sea salt
- ¼ teaspoon freshly ground black pepper
- 1 (6-pound) bone-in, skin-on turkey breast
- 1 cup dry white wine

Directions:

Preheat the oven to 325°F. Combine the olive oil, garlic, lemon zest, thyme, rosemary, parsley, mustard, sea salt, and pepper. Brush the herb mixture evenly over the surface of the turkey breast, and loosen the skin and rub underneath as well. Situate the turkey breast in a roasting pan on a rack, skin-side up.

Pour the wine in the pan. Roast for 1 to 1½ hours until the turkey reaches an internal temperature of 165 degrees F. Pull out from the oven and set separately for 20 minutes, tented with aluminum foil to keep it warm, before carving.

Nutrition (for 100g): 392 Calories 1g Fat 2g Carbohydrates 84g Protein 741mg Sodium

Chicken Sausage and Peppers

Preparation Time : 10 minutes

Cooking Time : 20 minutes

Servings : 6

Difficulty Level : Average

Ingredients:

- 2 tablespoons extra-virgin olive oil
- 6 Italian chicken sausage links
- 1 onion
- 1 red bell pepper
- 1 green bell pepper
- 3 garlic cloves, minced
- ½ cup dry white wine
- ½ teaspoon sea salt
- ¼ teaspoon freshly ground black pepper
- Pinch red pepper flakes

Directions:

Cook the olive oil on large skillet until it shimmers. Add the sausages and cook for 5 to 7 minutes, turning occasionally, until browned, and they reach an internal temperature of 165°F. With tongs, remove the sausage from the pan and set aside on a platter, tented with aluminum foil to keep warm.

Return the skillet to the heat and mix in the onion, red bell pepper, and green bell pepper. Cook and stir occasionally, until the vegetables begin to brown. Put in the garlic and cook for 30 seconds, stirring constantly.

Stir in the wine, sea salt, pepper, and red pepper flakes. Pull out and fold in any browned bits from the bottom of the pan. Simmer for about 4 minutes more, stirring, until the liquid reduces by half. Spoon the peppers over the sausages and serve.

Nutrition (for 100g): 173 Calories 1g Fat 6g Carbohydrates 22g Protein 582mg Sodium

Chicken Piccata

Preparation Time : 10 minutes

Cooking Time : 15 minutes

Servings : 6

Difficulty Level : Average

Ingredients:

- ½ cup whole-wheat flour
- ½ teaspoon sea salt
- 1/8 teaspoon freshly ground black pepper
- 1½ pounds chicken breasts, cut into 6 pieces
- 3 tablespoons extra-virgin olive oil
- 1 cup unsalted chicken broth
- ½ cup dry white wine
- Juice of 1 lemon
- Zest of 1 lemon
- ¼ cup capers, drained and rinsed
- ¼ cup chopped fresh parsley leaves

Directions:

In a shallow dish, whisk the flour, sea salt, and pepper. Scour the chicken in the flour and tap off any excess. Cook the olive oil until it shimmers.

Put the chicken and cook for about 4 minutes per side until browned. Pull out the chicken from the pan and set aside, tented with aluminum foil to keep warm.

Situate the skillet back to the heat and stir in the broth, wine, lemon juice, lemon zest, and capers. Use the side of a spoon scoop and fold in any browned bits from the pan's bottom. Simmer until the liquid thickens. Take out the skillet from the heat and take the chicken back to the pan. Turn to coat. Stir in the parsley and serve.

Nutrition (for 100g): 153 Calories 2g Fat 9g Carbohydrates 8g Protein 692mg Sodium

One-Pan Tuscan Chicken

Preparation Time : 10 minutes

Cooking Time : 25 minutes

Servings : 6

Difficulty Level : Difficult

Ingredients:

- ¼ cup extra-virgin olive oil, divided
- 1-pound boneless, skinless chicken breasts, cut into ¾-inch pieces
- 1 onion, chopped
- 1 red bell pepper, chopped
- 3 garlic cloves, minced
- ½ cup dry white wine
- 1 (14-ounce) can crushed tomatoes, undrained
- 1 (14-ounce) can chopped tomatoes, drained
- 1 (14-ounce) can white beans, drained
- 1 tablespoon dried Italian seasoning
- ½ teaspoon sea salt
- 1/8 teaspoon freshly ground black pepper
- 1/8 teaspoon red pepper flakes
- ¼ cup chopped fresh basil leaves

Directions:

Cook 2 tablespoons of olive oil until it shimmers. Mix in the chicken and cook until browned. Remove the chicken from the skillet and set aside on a platter, tented with aluminum foil to keep warm.

Situate the skillet back to the heat and heat up the remaining olive oil. Add the onion and red bell pepper. Cook and stir rarely, until the vegetables are soft. Put the garlic and cook for 30 seconds, stirring constantly.

Stir in the wine, and use the side of the spoon to scoop out any browned bits from the bottom of the pan. Cook for 1 minute, stirring.

Mix in the crushed and chopped tomatoes, white beans, Italian seasoning, sea salt, pepper, and red pepper flakes. Allow to simmer. Cook for 5 minutes, stirring occasionally.

Put the chicken back and any juices that have collected to the skillet. Cook until the chicken is cook through. Take out from the heat and stir in the basil before serving.

Nutrition (for 100g): 271 Calories 8g Fat 29g Carbohydrates 14g Protein 596mg Sodium

Chicken Kapama

Preparation Time : 10 minutes

Cooking Time : 2 hours

Servings : 4

Difficulty Level : Average

Ingredients:

- 1 (32-ounce) can chopped tomatoes, drained
- ¼ cup dry white wine
- 2 tablespoons tomato paste
- 3 tablespoons extra-virgin olive oil
- ¼ teaspoon red pepper flakes
- 1 teaspoon ground allspice
- ½ teaspoon dried oregano
- 2 whole cloves
- 1 cinnamon stick
- ½ teaspoon sea salt
- 1/8 teaspoon freshly ground black pepper
- 4 boneless, skinless chicken breast halves

Directions:

Mix the tomatoes, wine, tomato paste, olive oil, red pepper flakes, allspice, oregano, cloves, cinnamon stick, sea salt, and pepper in large pot. Bring to a simmer, stirring occasionally. Allow to simmer for 30 minutes, stirring occasionally. Remove and discard the whole cloves and cinnamon stick from the sauce and let the sauce cool.

Preheat the oven to 350°F. Situate the chicken in a 9-by-13-inch baking dish. Pour the sauce over the chicken and cover the pan with aluminum foil. Continue baking until it reaches 165°F internal temperature.

Nutrition (for 100g): 220 Calories 3g Fat 11g Carbohydrates 8g Protein 923mg Sodium

Spinach and Feta–Stuffed Chicken Breasts

Preparation Time : 10 minutes

Cooking Time : 45 minutes

Servings : 4

Difficulty Level : Average

Ingredients:

- 2 tablespoons extra-virgin olive oil
- 1-pound fresh baby spinach
- 3 garlic cloves, minced
- Zest of 1 lemon
- ½ teaspoon sea salt
- 1/8 teaspoon freshly ground black pepper
- ½ cup crumbled feta cheese
- 4 boneless, skinless chicken breasts

Directions:

Preheat the oven to 350°F. Cook the olive oil over medium heat until it shimmers. Add the spinach. Continue cooking and stirring, until wilted.

Stir in the garlic, lemon zest, sea salt, and pepper. Cook for 30 seconds, stirring constantly. Cool slightly and mix in the cheese.

Spread the spinach and cheese mixture in an even layer over the chicken pieces and roll the breast around the filling. Hold closed with toothpicks or butcher's twine. Place the breasts in a 9-by-13-

inch baking dish and bake for 30 to 40 minutes, or until the chicken have an internal temperature of 165°F. Take out from the oven and set aside for 5 minutes before slicing and serving.

Nutrition (for 100g): 263 Calories 3g Fat 7g Carbohydrates 17g Protein 639mg Sodium

Rosemary Baked Chicken Drumsticks

Preparation Time : 5 minutes

Cooking Time : 1 hour

Servings : 6

Difficulty Level : Easy

Ingredients:

- 2 tablespoons chopped fresh rosemary leaves
- 1 teaspoon garlic powder
- ½ teaspoon sea salt
- 1/8 teaspoon freshly ground black pepper
- Zest of 1 lemon
- 12 chicken drumsticks

Directions:

Preheat the oven to 350°F. Mix the rosemary, garlic powder, sea salt, pepper, and lemon zest.

Situate the drumsticks in a 9-by-13-inch baking dish and sprinkle with the rosemary mixture. Bake until the chicken reaches an internal temperature of 165°F.

Nutrition (for 100g): 163 Calories 1g Fat 2g Carbohydrates 26g Protein 633mg Sodium

Chicken with Onions, Potatoes, Figs, and Carrots

Preparation Time : 5 minutes

Cooking Time : 45 minutes

Servings : 4

Difficulty Level : Average

Ingredients:

- 2 cups fingerling potatoes, halved
- 4 fresh figs, quartered
- 2 carrots, julienned
- 2 tablespoons extra-virgin olive oil
- 1 teaspoon sea salt, divided
- ¼ teaspoon freshly ground black pepper
- 4 chicken leg-thigh quarters
- 2 tablespoons chopped fresh parsley leaves

Directions:

Preheat the oven to 425°F. In a small bowl, toss the potatoes, figs, and carrots with the olive oil, ½ teaspoon of sea salt, and the pepper. Spread in a 9-by-13-inch baking dish.

Season the chicken with the rest of t sea salt. Place it on top of the vegetables. Bake until the vegetables are soft and the chicken reaches an internal temperature of 165°F. Sprinkle with the parsley and serve.

Nutrition (for 100g): 429 Calories 4g Fat 27g Carbohydrates 52g Protein 581mg Sodium

Chicken Gyros with Tzatziki

Preparation Time : 15 minutes

Cooking Time : 1 hours and 20 minutes

Servings : 6

Difficulty Level : Average

Ingredients:

- 1-pound ground chicken breast
- 1 onion, grated with excess water wrung out
- 2 tablespoons dried rosemary
- 1 tablespoon dried marjoram
- 6 garlic cloves, minced
- ½ teaspoon sea salt
- ¼ teaspoon freshly ground black pepper
- Tzatziki Sauce

Directions:

Preheat the oven to 350°F. Mix the chicken, onion, rosemary, marjoram, garlic, sea salt, and pepper using food processor. Blend until the mixture forms a paste. Alternatively, mix these ingredients in a bowl until well combined (see preparation tip).

Press the mixture into a loaf pan. Bake until it reaches 165 degrees internal temperature. Take out from the oven and let rest for 20 minutes before slicing.

Slice the gyro and spoon the tzatziki sauce over the top.

Nutrition (for 100g): 289 Calories 1g Fat 20g Carbohydrates 50g Protein 622mg Sodium

Moussaka

Preparation Time : 10 minutes

Cooking Time : 45 minutes

Servings : 8

Difficulty Level : Difficult

Ingredients:

- 5 tablespoons extra-virgin olive oil, divided
- 1 eggplant, sliced (unpeeled)
- 1 onion, chopped
- 1 green bell pepper, seeded and chopped
- 1-pound ground turkey
- 3 garlic cloves, minced
- 2 tablespoons tomato paste
- 1 (14-ounce) can chopped tomatoes, drained
- 1 tablespoon Italian seasoning
- 2 teaspoons Worcestershire sauce
- 1 teaspoon dried oregano
- ½ teaspoon ground cinnamon
- 1 cup unsweetened nonfat plain Greek yogurt
- 1 egg, beaten
- ¼ teaspoon freshly ground black pepper
- ¼ teaspoon ground nutmeg
- ¼ cup grated Parmesan cheese
- 2 tablespoons chopped fresh parsley leaves

Directions:

Preheat the oven to 400°F. Cook 3 tablespoons of olive oil until it shimmers. Add the eggplant slices and brown for 3 to 4 minutes per side. Transfer to paper towels to drain.

Return the skillet to the heat and pour the remaining 2 tablespoons of olive oil. Add the onion and green bell pepper. Continue cooking until the vegetables are soft. Remove from the pan and set aside.

Pull out the skillet to the heat and stir in the turkey. Cook for about 5 minutes, crumbling with a spoon, until browned. Stir in the garlic and cook for 30 seconds, stirring constantly.

Stir in the tomato paste, tomatoes, Italian seasoning, Worcestershire sauce, oregano, and cinnamon. Place the onion and bell pepper back to the pan. Cook for 5 minutes, stirring. Combine the yogurt, egg, pepper, nutmeg, and cheese.

Arrange half of the meat mixture in a 9-by-13-inch baking dish. Layer with half the eggplant. Add the remaining meat mixture and the remaining eggplant. Spread with the yogurt mixture. Bake until golden brown. Garnish with the parsley and serve.

Nutrition (for 100g): 338 Calories 5g Fat 16g Carbohydrates 28g Protein 569mg Sodium

Dijon and Herb Pork Tenderloin

Preparation Time : 10 minutes

Cooking Time : 30 minutes

Servings : 6

Difficulty Level : Average

Ingredients:

- ½ cup fresh Italian parsley leaves, chopped
- 3 tablespoons fresh rosemary leaves, chopped
- 3 tablespoons fresh thyme leaves, chopped
- 3 tablespoons Dijon mustard
- 1 tablespoon extra-virgin olive oil
- 4 garlic cloves, minced
- ½ teaspoon sea salt
- ¼ teaspoon freshly ground black pepper
- 1 (1½-pound) pork tenderloin

Directions:

Preheat the oven to 400°F. Blend the parsley, rosemary, thyme, mustard, olive oil, garlic, sea salt, and pepper. Process for about 30 seconds until smooth. Spread the mixture evenly over the pork and place it on a rimmed baking sheet.

Bake until the meat reaches an internal temperature of 140°F. Pull out from the oven and set aside for 10 minutes before slicing and serving.

Nutrition (for 100g): 393 Calories 3g Fat 5g Carbohydrates 74g Protein 697mg Sodium

Steak with Red Wine–Mushroom Sauce

Preparation Time : minutes plus 8 hours to marinate

Cooking Time : 20 minutes

Servings : 4

Difficulty Level : Difficult

Ingredients:

- <u>For the Marinade and Steak</u>
- 1 cup dry red wine
- 3 garlic cloves, minced
- 2 tablespoons extra-virgin olive oil
- 1 tablespoon low-sodium soy sauce
- 1 tablespoon dried thyme
- 1 teaspoon Dijon mustard
- 2 tablespoons extra-virgin olive oil
- 1 to 1½ pounds skirt steak, flat iron steak, or tri-tip steak
- <u>For the Mushroom Sauce</u>
- 2 tablespoons extra-virgin olive oil
- 1-pound cremini mushrooms, quartered
- ½ teaspoon sea salt
- 1 teaspoon dried thyme
- 1/8 teaspoon freshly ground black pepper
- 2 garlic cloves, minced
- 1 cup dry red wine

Directions:

To Make the Marinade and Steak

In a small bowl, whisk the wine, garlic, olive oil, soy sauce, thyme, and mustard. Pour into a resealable bag and add the steak. Refrigerate the steak to marinate for 4 to 8 hours. Remove the steak from the marinade and pat it dry with paper towels.

Cook the olive oil in large pan until it shimmers.

Situate the steak and cook for about 4 minutes per side until deeply browned on each side and the steak reaches an internal temperature of 140°F. Remove the steak from the skillet and put it on a plate tented with aluminum foil to keep warm, while you prepare the mushroom sauce.

When the mushroom sauce is ready, slice the steak against the grain into ½-inch-thick slices.

To Make the Mushroom Sauce

Cook oil in the same skillet over medium-high heat. Add the mushrooms, sea salt, thyme, and pepper. Cook for about 6 minutes, stirring very infrequently, until the mushrooms are browned.

Sauté the garlic. Mix in the wine, and use the side of a wooden spoon to scoop out any browned bits from the bottom of the skillet. Cook until the liquid reduces by half. Serve the mushrooms spooned over the steak.

Nutrition (for 100g): 405 Calories 5g Fat 7g Carbohydrates 33g Protein 842mg Sodium

Greek Meatballs

Preparation Time : 20 minutes

Cooking Time : 25 minutes

Servings : 4

Difficulty Level : Average

Ingredients:

- 2 whole-wheat bread slices
- 1¼ pounds ground turkey
- 1 egg
- ¼ cup seasoned whole-wheat bread crumbs
- 3 garlic cloves, minced
- ¼ red onion, grated
- ¼ cup chopped fresh Italian parsley leaves
- 2 tablespoons chopped fresh mint leaves
- 2 tablespoons chopped fresh oregano leaves
- ½ teaspoon sea salt
- ¼ teaspoon freshly ground black pepper

Directions:

Preheat the oven to 350°F. Situate parchment paper or aluminum foil onto the baking sheet. Run the bread under water to wet it, and squeeze out any excess. Shred wet bread into small pieces and place it in a medium bowl.

Add the turkey, egg, bread crumbs, garlic, red onion, parsley, mint, oregano, sea salt, and pepper. Mix well. Form the mixture into ¼-cup-size balls. Place the meatballs on the prepared sheet and bake for about 25 minutes, or until the internal temperature reaches 165°F.

Nutrition (for 100g): 350 Calories 6g Fat 10g Carbohydrates 42g Protein 842mg Sodium

Lamb with String Beans

Preparation Time : 10 minutes

Cooking Time : 1 hour

Servings : 6

Difficulty Level : Difficult

Ingredients:

- ¼ cup extra-virgin olive oil, divided
- 6 lamb chops, trimmed of extra fat
- 1 teaspoon sea salt, divided
- ½ teaspoon freshly ground black pepper
- 2 tablespoons tomato paste
- 1½ cups hot water
- 1-pound green beans, trimmed and halved crosswise
- 1 onion, chopped
- 2 tomatoes, chopped

Directions:

Cook 2 tablespoons of olive oil in large skillet until it shimmers. Season the lamb chops with ½ teaspoon of sea salt and 1/8 teaspoon of pepper. Cook the lamb in the hot oil for about 4 minutes per side until browned on both sides. Situate the meat to a platter and set aside.

Position the skillet back to the heat and put the remaining 2 tablespoons of olive oil. Heat until it shimmers.

In a bowl, melt the tomato paste in the hot water. Add it to the hot skillet along with the green beans, onion, tomatoes, and the remaining ½ teaspoon of sea salt and ¼ teaspoon of pepper. Bring to a simmer, using a spoon's side to scrape browned bits from the bottom of the pan.

Return the lamb chops to the pan. Allow to boil and adjust the heat to medium-low. Simmer for 45 minutes until the beans are soft, adding additional water as needed to adjust the sauce's thickness.

Nutrition (for 100g): 439 Calories 4g Fat 10g Carbohydrates 50g Protein 745mg Sodium

Chicken in Tomato-Balsamic Pan Sauce

Preparation Time : 10 minutes

Cooking Time : 20 minutes

Servings : 4

Difficulty Level : Average

Ingredients

- 2 (8 oz. or 226.7 g each) boneless chicken breasts, skinless
- ½ tsp. salt
- ½ tsp. ground pepper
- 3 tbsps. extra-virgin olive oil
- ½ c. halved cherry tomatoes
- 2 tbsps. sliced shallot
- ¼ c. balsamic vinegar
- 1 tbsp. minced garlic
- 1 tbsp. toasted fennel seeds, crushed
- 1 tbsp. butter

Directions:

Slice the chicken breasts into 4 pieces and beat them with a mallet till it reaches a thickness of a ¼ inch. Use ¼ teaspoons of pepper and salt to coat the chicken. Heat two tablespoons of oil in a skillet and keep the heat to a medium. Cook the chicken breasts on both sides for three minutes. Place it to a serving plate and cover it with foil to keep it warm.

Add one tablespoon oil, shallot, and tomatoes in a pan and cook till it softens. Add vinegar and boil the mix till the vinegar gets reduced by half. Put fennel seeds, garlic, salt, and pepper and cook for about four minutes. Pull it out from the heat and stir it with butter. Pour this sauce over chicken and serve.

Nutrition (for 100g): 294 Calories 17g Fat 10g Carbohydrates 2g Protein 639mg Sodium

Brown Rice, Feta, Fresh Pea, and Mint Salad

Preparation Time : 10 minutes

Cooking Time : 25 minutes

Servings : 4

Difficulty Level : Easy

Ingredients:

- 2 c. brown rice
- 3 c. water
- Salt
- 5 oz. or 141.7 g crumbled feta cheese
- 2 c. cooked peas
- ½ c. chopped mint, fresh
- 2 tbsps. olive oil
- Salt and pepper

Directions:

Place the brown rice, water, and salt into a saucepan over medium heat, cover, and bring to boiling point. Turn the lower heat and allow it to cook until the water has dissolved and the rice is soft but chewy. Leave to cool completely

Add the feta, peas, mint, olive oil, salt, and pepper to a salad bowl with the cooled rice and toss to combine Serve and enjoy!

Nutrition (for 100g): 613 Calories 18.2g Fat 45g Carbohydrates 12g Protein 755mg Sodium

Whole Grain Pita Bread Stuffed with Olives and Chickpeas

Preparation Time : 10 minutes

Cooking Time : 20 minutes

Servings : 2

Difficulty Level : Average

Ingredients:

- 2 wholegrain pita pockets
- 2 tbsps. olive oil
- 2 garlic cloves, chopped
- 1 onion, chopped
- ½ tsp. cumin
- 10 black olives, chopped
- 2 c. cooked chickpeas
- Salt and pepper

Directions:

Slice open the pita pockets and set aside Adjust your heat to medium and set a pan in place. Add in the olive oil and heat. Mix in the garlic, onion, and cumin to the hot pan and stir as the onions soften and the cumin is fragrant Add the olives, chickpeas, salt, and pepper and toss everything together until the chickpeas become golden

Set the pan from heat and use your wooden spoon to roughly mash the chickpeas so that some are intact and some are crushed Heat your pita pockets in the microwave, in the oven, or on a clean pan on the stove

Fill them with your chickpea mixture and enjoy!

Nutrition (for 100g): 503 Calories 19g Fat 14g Carbohydrates 15.7g Protein 798mg Sodium

Roasted Carrots with Walnuts and Cannellini Beans

Preparation Time : 10 minutes

Cooking Time : 45 minutes

Servings : 4

Difficulty Level : Average

Ingredients:

- 4 peeled carrots, chopped
- 1 c. walnuts
- 1 tbsp. honey
- 2 tbsps. olive oil
- 2 c. canned cannellini beans, drained
- 1 fresh thyme sprig
- Salt and pepper

Directions:

Set oven to 400 F/204 C and line a baking tray or roasting pan with baking paper Lay the carrots and walnuts onto the lined tray or pan Sprinkle olive oil and honey over the carrots and walnuts and give everything a rub to make sure each piece is coated Scatter the beans onto the tray and nestle into the carrots and walnuts

Add the thyme and sprinkle everything with salt and pepper Set tray in your oven and roast for about 40 minutes.

Serve and enjoy

Nutrition (for 100g): 385 Calories 27g Fat 6g Carbohydrates 18g Protein 859mg Sodium

Seasoned Buttered Chicken

Preparation Time : 10 minutes

Cooking Time : 25 minutes

Servings : 4

Difficulty Level : Average

Ingredients:

- ½ c. Heavy Whipping Cream
- 1 tbsp. Salt
- ½ c. Bone Broth
- 1 tbsp. Pepper
- 4 tbsps. Butter
- 4 Chicken Breast Halves

Directions:

Place cooking pan on your oven over medium heat and add in one tablespoon of butter. Once the butter is warm and melted, place the chicken in and cook for five minutes on either side. At the end of this time, the chicken should be cooked through and golden; if it is, go ahead and place it on a plate.

Next, you are going to add the bone broth into the warm pan. Add heavy whipping cream, salt, and pepper. Then, leave the pan alone until your sauce begins to simmer. Allow this process to happen for five minutes to let the sauce thicken up.

Finally, you are going to add the rest of your butter and the chicken back into the pan. Be sure to use a spoon to place the sauce over your chicken and smother it completely. Serve

Nutrition (for 100g): 350 Calories 25g Fat 10g Carbohydrates 25g Protein 869mg Sodium

Double Cheesy Bacon Chicken

Preparation Time : 10 minutes

Cooking Time : 30 minutes

Servings : 4

Difficulty Level : Easy

Ingredients:

- 4 oz. or 113 g. Cream Cheese
- 1 c. Cheddar Cheese
- 8 strips Bacon
- Sea salt
- Pepper
- 2 Garlic cloves, finely chopped
- Chicken Breast
- 1 tbsp. Bacon Grease or Butter

Directions:

Ready the oven to 400 F/204 C Slice the chicken breasts in half to make them thin

Season with salt, pepper, and garlic Grease a baking pan with butter and place chicken breasts into it. Add the cream cheese and cheddar cheese on top of the breasts

Add bacon slices as well Place the pan to the oven for 30 minutes Serve hot

Nutrition (for 100g): 610 Calories 32g Fat 3g Carbohydrates 38g Protein 759mg Sodium

Shrimps with Lemon and Pepper

Preparation Time : 10 minutes

Cooking Time : 10 minutes

Servings : 4

Difficulty Level : Easy

Ingredients:

- 40 deveined shrimps, peeled
- 6 minced garlic cloves
- Salt and black pepper
- 3 tbsps. olive oil
- ¼ tsp. sweet paprika
- A pinch crushed red pepper flake
- ¼ tsp. grated lemon zest
- 3 tbsps. Sherry or another wine
- 1½ tbsps. sliced chives
- Juice of 1 lemon

Directions:

Adjust your heat to medium-high and set a pan in place.

Add oil and shrimp, sprinkle with pepper and salt and cook for 1 minute Add paprika, garlic and pepper flakes, stir and cook for 1 minute. Gently stir in sherry and allow to cook for an extra minute

Take shrimp off the heat, add chives and lemon zest, stir and transfer shrimp to plates. Add lemon juice all over and serve

Nutrition (for 100g): 140 Calories 1g Fat 5g Carbohydrates 18g Protein 694mg Sodium

Breaded and Spiced Halibut

Preparation Time : 5 minutes

Cooking Time : 25 minutes

Servings : 4

Difficulty Level : Easy

Ingredients:

- ¼ c. chopped fresh chives
- ¼ c. chopped fresh dill
- ¼ tsp. ground black pepper
- ¾ c. panko breadcrumbs
- 1 tbsp. extra-virgin olive oil
- 1 tsp. finely grated lemon zest
- 1 tsp. sea salt
- 1/3 c. chopped fresh parsley
- 4 (6 oz. or 170 g. each) halibut fillets

Directions:

In a medium bowl, mix olive oil and the rest ingredients except halibut fillets and breadcrumbs

Place halibut fillets into the mixture and marinate for 30 minutes Preheat your oven to 400 F/204 C Set a foil to a baking sheet, grease with cooking spray Dip the fillets to the breadcrumbs and put to the baking sheet Cook in the oven for 20 minutes Serve hot

Nutrition (for 100g): 667 Calories 24.5g Fat 2g Carbohydrates 54.8g Protein 756mg Sodium

Curry Salmon with Mustard

Preparation Time : 10 minutes

Cooking Time : 20 minutes

Servings : 4

Difficulty Level : Easy

Ingredients:

- ¼ tsp. ground red pepper or chili powder
- ¼ tsp. turmeric, ground
- ¼ tsp. salt
- 1 tsp. honey
- ¼ tsp. garlic powder
- 2 tsps. whole grain mustard
- 4 (6 oz. or 170 g. each) salmon fillets

Directions:

In a bowl mix mustard and the rest ingredients except salmon Preheat the oven to 350 F/176 C Grease a baking dish with cooking spray. Place salmon on baking dish with skin side down and spread evenly mustard mixture on top of fillets Place into the oven and cook for 10-15 minutes or until flaky

Nutrition (for 100g): 324 Calories 18.9g Fat 1.3g Carbohydrates 34g Protein 593mg Sodium

Walnut-Rosemary Crusted Salmon

Preparation Time : 10 minutes

Cooking Time : 25 minutes

Servings : 4

Difficulty Level : Average

Ingredients:

- 1 lb. or 450 g. frozen skinless salmon fillet
- 2 tsps. Dijon mustard
- 1 clove garlic, minced
- ¼ tsp. lemon zest
- ½ tsp. honey
- ½ tsp. kosher salt
- 1 tsp. freshly chopped rosemary
- 3 tbsps. panko breadcrumbs
- ¼ tsp. crushed red pepper
- 3 tbsps. chopped walnuts
- 2 tsp. extra-virgin olive oil

Directions:

Prepare the oven to 420 F/215 C and use parchment paper to line a rimmed baking sheet. In a bowl combine mustard, lemon zest, garlic, lemon juice, honey, rosemary, crushed red pepper, and salt. In another bowl mix walnut, panko, and 1 tsp oil Place parchments paper on the baking sheet and lay the salmon on it

Spread mustard mixture on the fish, and top with the panko mixture. Spray the rest of olive oil lightly on the salmon. Bake for about 10 -12 minutes or until the salmon is being separated by a fork Serve hot

Nutrition (for 100g): 222 Calories 12g Fat 4g Carbohydrates 0.8g Protein 812mg Sodium

Quick Tomato Spaghetti

Preparation Time : 10 minutes

Cooking Time : 25 minutes

Servings : 4

Difficulty Level : Average

Ingredients:

- 8 oz. or 226.7g spaghetti
- 3 tbsps. olive oil
- 4 garlic cloves, sliced
- 1 jalapeno, sliced
- 2 c. cherry tomatoes
- Salt and pepper
- 1 tsp. balsamic vinegar
- ½ c. Parmesan, grated

Directions:

Boil a large pot of water on medium flame. Add a pinch of salt and bring to a boil then add the spaghetti. Allow cooking for 8 minutes. While the pasta cooks, heat the oil in a skillet and add the garlic and jalapeno. Cook for an extra 1 minute then stir in the tomatoes, pepper, and salt.

Cook for 5-7 minutes until the tomatoes' skins burst.

Add the vinegar and remove off heat. Drain spaghetti well and mix it with the tomato sauce. Sprinkle with cheese and serve right away.

Nutrition (for 100g): 298 Calories 13.5g Fat 10.5g Carbohydrates 8g Protein 749mg Sodium

Chili Oregano Baked Cheese

Preparation Time : 10 minutes

Cooking Time : 25 minutes

Servings : 4

Difficulty Level : Easy

Ingredients:

- 8 oz. or 226.7g feta cheese
- 4 oz. or 113g mozzarella, crumbled
- 1 sliced chili pepper
- 1 tsp. dried oregano
- 2 tbsps. olive oil

Directions:

Place the feta cheese in a small deep-dish baking pan. Top with the mozzarella then season with pepper slices and oregano. cover your pan with lid. Bake in the preheated oven at 350 F/176 C for 20 minutes. Serve the cheese and enjoy it.

Nutrition (for 100g): 292 Calories 24.2g Fat 5.7g Carbohydrates 2g Protein 733mg Sodium

311. Crispy Italian Chicken

Preparation Time : 10 minutes

Cooking Time : 30 minutes

Servings : 4

Difficulty Level : Easy

Ingredients:

- 4 chicken legs
- 1 tsp. dried basil
- 1 tsp. dried oregano
- Salt and pepper
- 3 tbsps. olive oil
- 1 tbsp. balsamic vinegar

Directions:

Season the chicken well with basil, and oregano. Using a skillet, add oil and heat. Add the chicken in the hot oil. Let each side cook for 5 minutes until golden then cover the skillet with a lid.

Adjust your heat to medium and cook for 10 minutes on one side then flip the chicken repeatedly, cooking for another 10 minutes until crispy. Serve the chicken and enjoy.

Nutrition (for 100g): 262 Calories 13.9g Fat 11g Carbohydrates 32.6g Protein 693mg Sodium

Sea Bass in a Pocket

Preparation Time : 10 minutes

Cooking Time : 25 minutes

Servings : 4

Difficulty Level : Average

Ingredients:

- 4 sea bass fillets
- 4 sliced garlic cloves
- 1 sliced celery stalk
- 1 sliced zucchini
- 1 c. halved cherry tomatoes halved
- 1 shallot, sliced
- 1 tsp. dried oregano
- Salt and pepper

Directions:

Mix the garlic, celery, zucchini, tomatoes, shallot, and oregano in a bowl. Add salt and pepper to taste. Take 4 sheets of baking paper and arrange them on your working surface. Spoon the vegetable mixture in the center of each sheet.

Top with a fish fillet then wrap the paper well so it resembles a pocket. Place the wrapped fish in a baking tray and cook in the preheated oven at 350 F/176 C for 15 minutes. Serve the fish warm and fresh.

Nutrition (for 100g): 149 Calories 2.8g Fat 5.2g Carbohydrates 25.2g Protein 696mg Sodium

Creamy Smoked Salmon Pasta

Preparation Time : 5 minutes

Cooking Time : 35 minutes

Servings : 4

Difficulty Level : Average

Ingredients:

- 2 tbsps. olive oil
- 2 chopped garlic cloves
- 1 shallot, chopped
- 4 oz. or 113 g chopped salmon, smoked
- 1 c. green peas
- 1 c. heavy cream
- Salt and pepper
- 1 pinch chili flakes
- 8 oz. or 230 g penne pasta
- 6 c. water

Directions:

Place skillet on medium-high heat and add oil. Add the garlic and shallot. Cook for 5 minutes or until softened. Add peas, salt, pepper, and chili flakes. Cook for 10 minutes

Add the salmon, and continue cooking for 5-7 minutes more. Add heavy cream, reduce heat and cook for an extra 5 minutes.

In the meantime, place a pan with water and salt to your taste on high heat as soon as it boils, add penne pasta and cook for 8-10 minutes or until softened Drain the pasta, add to the salmon sauce and serve

Nutrition (for 100g): 393 Calories 20.8g Fat 38g Carbohydrates 3g Protein 836mg Sodium

Slow Cooker Greek Chicken

Preparation Time : 20 minutes

Cooking Time : 3 hours

Servings : 4

Difficulty Level : Average

Ingredients:

- 1 tablespoon extra-virgin olive oil
- 2 pounds boneless, chicken breasts
- ½ tsp kosher salt
- ¼ tsp black pepper
- 1 (12-ounce) jar roasted red peppers
- 1 cup Kalamata olives
- 1 medium red onion, cut into chunks
- 3 tablespoons red wine vinegar
- 1 tablespoon minced garlic
- 1 teaspoon honey
- 1 teaspoon dried oregano
- 1 teaspoon dried thyme
- ½ cup feta cheese (optional, for serving)
- Chopped fresh herbs: any mix of basil, parsley, or thyme (optional, for serving)

Directions:

Brush slow cooker with nonstick cooking spray or olive oil. Cook the olive oil in a large skillet. Season both side of the chicken breasts. Once the oil is hot, add the chicken breasts and sear on both sides (about 3 minutes).

Once cooked, transfer it to the slow cooker. Add the red peppers, olives, and red onion to the chicken breasts. Try to place the vegetables around the chicken and not directly on top.

In a small bowl, mix the vinegar, garlic, honey, oregano, and thyme. Once combined, pour it over the chicken. Cook the chicken on low for 3 hours or until no longer pink in the middle. Serve with crumbled feta cheese and fresh herbs.

Nutrition (for 100g): 399 Calories 17g Fat 12g Carbohydrates 50g Protein 793mg Sodium

Chicken Gyros

Preparation Time : 10 minutes

Cooking Time : 4 hours

Servings : 4

Difficulty Level : Average

Ingredients:

- 2 lbs. boneless chicken breasts or chicken tenders
- Juice of one lemon
- 3 cloves garlic
- 2 teaspoons red wine vinegar
- 2–3 tablespoons olive oil
- ½ cup Greek yogurt
- 2 teaspoons dried oregano
- 2–4 teaspoons Greek seasoning
- ½ small red onion, chopped
- 2 tablespoons dill weed
- Tzatziki Sauce
- 1 cup plain Greek yogurt
- 1 tablespoon dill weed
- 1 small English cucumber, chopped
- Pinch of salt and pepper
- 1 teaspoon onion powder
- For Toppings:

* Tomatoes

* Chopped cucumbers

* Chopped red onion

* Diced feta cheese

* Crumbled pita bread

Directions:

Slice the chicken breasts into cubes and place in the slow cooker. Add the lemon juice, garlic, vinegar, olive oil, Greek yogurt, oregano, Greek seasoning, red onion, and dill to the slow cooker and stir to make sure everything is well combined.

Cook on low for 5–6 hours or on high for 2–3 hours. In the meantime, incorporate all ingredients for the tzatziki sauce and stir. When well mixed, put in the refrigerator until the chicken is done.

When the chicken has finished cooking, serve with pita bread and any or all of the toppings listed above.

Nutrition (for 100g): 317 Calories 7.4g Fat 36.1g Carbohydrates 28.6g Protein 476mg Sodium

Slow Cooker Chicken Cassoulet

Preparation Time : 10 minutes

Cooking Time : 20 minutes

Servings : 16

Difficulty Level : Average

Ingredients:

- 1 cup dry navy beans, soaked
- 8 bone-in skinless chicken thighs
- 1 Polish sausage, cooked and chopped into bite-sized pieces (optional)
- 1¼ cup tomato juice
- 1 (28-ounce) can halved tomatoes
- 1 tbsp Worcestershire sauce
- 1 tsp instant beef or chicken bouillon granules
- ½ tsp dried basil
- ½ teaspoon dried oregano
- ½ teaspoon paprika
- ½ cup chopped celery
- ½ cup chopped carrot
- ½ cup chopped onion

Directions:

Brush the slow cooker with olive oil or nonstick cooking spray. In a mixing bowl, stir together the tomato juice, tomatoes, Worcestershire sauce, beef bouillon, basil, oregano, and paprika. Make sure the ingredients are well combined.

Place the chicken and sausage into the slow cooker and cover with the tomato juice mixture. Top with celery, carrot, and onion. Cook on low for 10–12 hours.

Nutrition (for 100g): 244 Calories 7g Fat 25g Carbohydrates 21g

Slow Cooker Chicken Provencal

Preparation Time : 5 minutes

Cooking Time : 8 hours

Servings : 4

Difficulty Level : Easy

Ingredients:

- 4 (6-ounce) skinless bone-in chicken breast halves
- 2 teaspoons dried basil
- 1 teaspoon dried thyme
- 1/8 teaspoon salt
- 1/8 teaspoon freshly ground black pepper
- 1 yellow pepper, diced
- 1 red pepper, diced
- 1 (15.5-ounce) can cannellini beans
- 1 (14.5-ounce) can petite tomatoes with basil, garlic, and oregano, undrained

Directions:

Brush the slow cooker with nonstick olive oil. Add all the ingredients to the slow cooker and stir to combine. Cook on low for 8 hours.

Nutrition (for 100g): 304 Calories 4.5g Fat 27.3g Carbohydrates 39.4g Protein 639mg Sodium

Greek Style Turkey Roast

Preparation Time : 20 minutes

Cooking Time : 7 hours and 30 minutes

Servings : 8

Difficulty Level : Average

Ingredients:

- 1 (4-pound) boneless turkey breast, trimmed
- ½ cup chicken broth, divided
- 2 tablespoons fresh lemon juice
- 2 cups chopped onion
- ½ cup pitted Kalamata olives
- ½ cup oil-packed sun-dried tomatoes, thinly sliced
- 1 teaspoon Greek seasoning
- ½ teaspoon salt
- ¼ teaspoon fresh ground black pepper
- 3 tablespoons all-purpose flour (or whole wheat)

Directions:

Brush the slow cooker with nonstick cooking spray or olive oil.
Add the turkey, ¼ cup of the chicken broth, lemon juice, onion,
olives, sun-dried tomatoes, Greek seasoning, salt and pepper to the
slow cooker.

Cook on low for 7 hours. Scourge the flour into the remaining ¼ cup of chicken broth, then stir gently into the slow cooker. Cook for an additional 30 minutes.

Nutrition (for 100g): 341 Calories 19g Fat 12g Carbohydrates 36.4g Protein 639mg Sodium

Garlic Chicken with Couscous

Preparation Time : 25 minutes

Cooking Time : 7 hours

Servings : 4

Difficulty Level : Average

Ingredients:

- 1 whole chicken, cut into pieces
- 1 tablespoon extra-virgin olive oil
- 6 cloves garlic, halved
- 1 cup dry white wine
- 1 cup couscous
- ½ teaspoon salt
- ½ teaspoon pepper
- 1 medium onion, thinly sliced
- 2 teaspoons dried thyme
- 1/3 cup whole wheat flour

Directions:

Cook the olive oil in a heavy skillet. When skillet is hot, add the chicken to sear. Make sure the chicken pieces don't touch each other. Cook with the skin side down for about 3 minutes or until browned.

Brush your slow cooker with nonstick cooking spray or olive oil. Put the onion, garlic, and thyme into the slow cooker and sprinkle with salt and pepper. Stir in the chicken on top of the onions.

In a separate bowl, whisk the flour into the wine until there are no lumps, then pour over the chicken. Cook on low for 7 hours or until done. You can cook on high for 3 hours as well. Serve the chicken over the cooked couscous and spoon sauce over the top.

Nutrition (for 100g): 440 Calories 17.5g Fat 14g Carbohydrates 35.8g Protein 674mg Sodium

Chicken Karahi

Preparation Time : 5 minutes

Cooking Time : 5 hours

Servings : 4

Difficulty Level : Easy

Ingredients:

- 2 lbs. chicken breasts or thighs
- ¼ cup olive oil
- 1 small can tomato paste
- 1 tablespoon butter
- 1 large onion, diced
- ½ cup plain Greek yogurt
- ½ cup water
- 2 tablespoons ginger in garlic paste
- 3 tablespoons fenugreek leaves
- 1 teaspoon ground coriander
- 1 medium tomato
- 1 teaspoon red chili
- 2 green chilies
- 1 teaspoon turmeric
- 1 tablespoon garam masala
- 1 teaspoon cumin powder
- 1 teaspoon sea salt
- ¼ teaspoon nutmeg

Directions:

Brush the slow cooker with nonstick cooking spray. In a small bowl, thoroughly mix all of the spices. Mix in the chicken to the slow cooker, followed by the ingredients' rest, including the spice mixture. Stir until everything is well mixed with the spices.

Cook on low for 4–5 hours. Serve with naan or Italian bread.

Nutrition (for 100g): 345 Calories 9.9g Fat 10g Carbohydrates 53.7g Protein 715mg Sodium

Chicken Cacciatore with Orzo

Preparation Time : 20 minutes

Cooking Time : 4 hours

Servings : 6

Difficulty Level : Easy

Ingredients:

- 2 pounds skin-on chicken thighs
- 1 tablespoon olive oil
- 1 cup mushrooms, quartered
- 3 carrots, chopped
- 1 small jar Kalamata olives
- 2 (14-ounce) cans diced tomatoes
- 1 small can tomato paste
- 1 cup red wine
- 5 garlic cloves
- 1 cup orzo

Directions:

In a large skillet, cook the olive oil. When the oil is heated, add the chicken, skin side down, and sear it. Make sure the pieces of chicken don't touch each other.

When the chicken is browned, add to the slow cooker along with all the ingredients except the orzo. Cook the chicken on low for 2 hours, then add the orzo and cook for an additional 2 hours. Serve with a crusty French bread.

Nutrition (for 100g): 424 Calories 16g Fat 10g Carbohydrates 11g Protein 845mg Sodium

Slow Cooked Daube Provencal

Preparation Time : 15 minutes

Cooking Time : 8 hours

Servings : 8

Difficulty Level : Average

Ingredients:

- 1 tablespoon olive oil
- 10 garlic cloves, minced
- 2 pounds boneless chuck roast
- 1½ teaspoons salt, divided
- ½ teaspoon freshly ground black pepper
- 1 cup dry red wine
- 2 cups carrots, chopped
- 1½ cups onion, chopped
- ½ cup beef broth
- 1 (14-ounce) can diced tomatoes
- 1 tablespoon tomato paste
- 1 teaspoon fresh rosemary, chopped
- 1 teaspoon fresh thyme, chopped
- ½ teaspoon orange zest, grated
- ½ teaspoon ground cinnamon
- ¼ teaspoon ground cloves
- 1 bay leaf

Directions:

Preheat a skillet and then add the olive oil. Add the minced garlic and onions and cook until the onions are soft and the garlic begins to brown.

Add the cubed meat, salt, and pepper and cook until the meat has browned. Transfer the meat to the slow cooker. Mix in the beef broth to the skillet and let simmer for about 3 minutes to deglaze the pan, then pour into slow cooker over the meat.

Incorporate the rest of the ingredients to the slow cooker and stir well to combine. Adjust slow cooker to low and cook for 8 hours, or set to high and cook for 4 hours. Serve with a side of egg noodles, rice or some crusty Italian bread.

Nutrition (for 100g): 547 Calories 30.5g Fat 22g Carbohydrates 45.2g Protein 809mg Sodium

Osso Bucco

Preparation Time : 30 minutes

Cooking Time : 8 hours

Servings : 3

Difficulty Level : Average

Ingredients:

- 4 beef shanks or veal shanks
- 1 teaspoon sea salt
- ½ teaspoon ground black pepper
- 3 tablespoons whole wheat flour
- 1–2 tablespoons olive oil
- 2 medium onions, diced
- 2 medium carrots, diced
- 2 celery stalks, diced
- 4 garlic cloves, minced
- 1 (14-ounce) can diced tomatoes
- 2 teaspoons dried thyme leaves
- ½ cup beef or vegetable stock

Directions:

Season the shanks on both sides, then dip in the flour to coat. Heat a large skillet over high heat. Add the olive oil. Once the oil is hot, add the shanks and brown evenly on both sides. When browned, transfer to the slow cooker.

Pour the stock into the skillet and let simmer for 3–5 minutes while stirring to deglaze the pan. Transfer the rest of the ingredients to the slow cooker and pour the stock from the skillet over the top.

Adjust the slow cooker to low and cook for 8 hours. Serve the Osso Bucco over quinoa, brown rice, or even cauliflower rice.

Nutrition (for 100g): 589 Calories 21.3g Fat 15g Carbohydrates 74.7g Protein 893mg Sodium

Slow Cooker Beef Bourguignon

Preparation Time : 5 minutes

Cooking Time : 8 hours

Servings : 8

Difficulty Level : Difficult

Ingredients:

- 1 tablespoon extra-virgin olive oil
- 6 ounces bacon, roughly chopped
- 3 pounds beef brisket, trimmed of fat, cut into 2-inch cubes
- 1 large carrot, sliced
- 1 large white onion, diced
- 6 cloves garlic, minced and divided
- ½ teaspoon coarse salt
- ½ teaspoon freshly ground pepper
- 2 tablespoons whole wheat
- 12 small pearl onions
- 3 cups red wine (Merlot, Pinot Noir, or Chianti)
- 2 cups beef stock
- 2 tablespoons tomato paste
- 1 beef bouillon cube, crushed
- 1 teaspoon fresh thyme, finely chopped
- 2 tablespoons fresh parsley
- 2 bay leaves
- 2 tablespoons butter or 1 tablespoon olive oil

- 1 pound fresh small white or brown mushrooms, quartered

Directions:

Heat up a skillet over medium-high heat, then add the olive oil. When the oil has heated, cook the bacon until it is crisp, then place it in your slow cooker. Save the bacon fat in the skillet.

Pat dry the beef and cook it in the same skillet with the bacon fat until all sides have the same brown coloring. Transfer to the slow cooker.

Mix in the onions and carrots to the slow cooker and season with the salt and pepper. Stir to combine the ingredients and make sure everything is seasoned.

Stir in the red wine into the skillet and simmer for 4–5 minutes to deglaze the pan, then whisk in the flour, stirring until smooth. Continue cooking until the liquid reduces and thickens a bit.

When the liquid has thickened, pour it into the slow cooker and stir to coat everything with the wine mixture. Add the tomato paste, bouillon cube, thyme, parsley, 4 cloves of garlic, and bay leaf. Adjust your slow cooker to high and cook for 6 hours, or set to low and cook for 8 hours.

Soften the butter or heat the olive oil in a skillet over medium heat. When the oil is hot, stir in the remaining 2 cloves of garlic and cook for about 1 minute before adding the mushrooms. Cook the mushrooms until soft, then add to the slow cooker and mix to combine.

Serve with mashed potatoes, rice or noodles.

Nutrition (for 100g): 672 Calories 32g Fat 15g Carbohydrates 56g Protein 693mg Sodium

Balsamic Beef

Preparation Time : 5 minutes

Cooking Time : 8 hours

Servings : 10

Difficulty Level : Average

Ingredients:

- 2 pounds boneless chuck roast
- 1 tablespoon olive oil
- Rub
- 1 teaspoon garlic powder
- ½ teaspoon onion powder
- 1 teaspoon sea salt
- ½ teaspoon freshly ground black pepper
- Sauce
- ½ cup balsamic vinegar
- 2 tablespoons honey
- 1 tablespoon honey mustard
- 1 cup beef broth
- 1 tablespoon tapioca, whole wheat flour, or cornstarch (to thicken sauce when it is done cooking if desired)

Directions:

Incorporate all of the ingredients for the rub.

In a separate bowl, mix the balsamic vinegar, honey, honey mustard, and beef broth. Coat the roast in olive oil, then rub in the spices from the rub mix. Place the roast in the slow cooker and then pour the sauce over the top. Adjust the slow cooker to low and cook for 8 hours.

If you want to thicken the sauce when the roast is done cooking transfer it from the slow cooker to a serving plate. Then fill the liquid into a saucepan and heat to boiling on the stovetop. Mix the flour until smooth and let simmer until the sauce thickens.

Nutrition (for 100g): 306 Calories 19g Fat 13g Carbohydrates 25g Protein 823mg Sodium

Veal Pot Roast

Preparation Time : 20 minutes

Cooking Time : 5 hours

Servings : 8

Difficulty Level : Average

Ingredients:

- 2 tablespoons olive oil
- Salt and pepper
- 3-pound boneless veal roast, tied
- 4 medium carrots, peeled
- 2 parsnips, peeled and halved
- 2 white turnips, peeled and quartered
- 10 garlic cloves, peeled
- 2 sprigs fresh thyme
- 1 orange, scrubbed and zested
- 1 cup chicken or veal stock

Directions:

Heat a large skillet over medium-high heat. Scour veal roast all over with olive oil, then season with salt and pepper. When the skillet is hot, add the veal roast and sear on all sides. This will take about 3 minutes on every side, but this process seals in the juices and makes the meat succulent.

When cooked, place it to the slow cooker. Toss the carrots, parsnips, turnips, and garlic into the skillet. Stir and cook for about 5 minutes—not all the way through, just to get some of the brown bits from the veal and give them a bit of color.

Transfer the vegetables to the slow cooker, placing them all around the meat. Top the roast with the thyme and the zest from the orange. Cut the orange in half and squeeze the juice over the top of the meat. Add the chicken stock, then cook the roast on low for 5 hours.

Nutrition (for 100g): 426 Calories 12.8g Fat 10g Carbohydrates 48.8g Protein 822mg Sodium

Mediterranean Rice and Sausage

Preparation Time : 15 minutes

Cooking Time : 8 hours

Servings : 6

Difficulty Level : Average

Ingredients:

- 1½ pounds Italian sausage, crumbled
- 1 medium onion, chopped
- 2 tablespoons steak sauce
- 2 cups long grain rice, uncooked
- 1 (14-ounce) can diced tomatoes with juice
- ½ cup water
- 1 medium green pepper, diced

Directions:

Spray your slow cooker with olive oil or nonstick cooking spray. Add the sausage, onion, and steak sauce to the slow cooker. Set on low for 8 to 10 hours.

After 8 hours, add the rice, tomatoes, water and green pepper. Stir to combine thoroughly. Cook an additional 20 to 25 minutes.

Nutrition (for 100g): 650 Calories 36g Fat 11g Carbohydrates 22g Protein 633mg Sodium

Spanish Meatballs

Preparation Time : 20 minutes

Cooking Time : 5 hours

Servings : 6

Difficulty Level : Difficult

Ingredients:

- 1-pound ground turkey
- 1-pound ground pork
- 2 eggs
- 1 (20-ounce) can diced tomatoes
- ¾ cup sweet onion, minced, divided
- ¼ cup plus 1 tablespoon breadcrumbs
- 3 tablespoons fresh parsley, chopped
- 1½ teaspoons cumin
- 1½ teaspoons paprika (sweet or hot)

Directions:

Spray the slow cooker with olive oil.

In a mixing bowl, incorporate the ground meat, eggs, about half of the onions, the breadcrumbs, and the spices.

Wash your hands and mix together until everything is well combined. Do not over-mix, though, as this makes for tough meatballs. Shape into meatballs. How big you make them will obviously determine how many total meatballs you get.

In a skillet, cook 2 tablespoons of olive oil over medium heat. Once hot, mix in the meatballs and brown on all sides. Make sure the balls aren't touching each other so they brown evenly. Once done, transfer them to the slow cooker.

Add the rest of the onions and the tomatoes to the skillet and allow them to cook for a few minutes, scraping the brown bits from the meatballs up to add flavor. Transfer the tomatoes over the meatballs in the slow cooker and cook on low for 5 hours.

Nutrition (for 100g): 372 Calories 21.7g Fat 15g Carbohydrates 28.6 Protein 772mg Sodium

Cauliflower Steaks with Olive Citrus Sauce

Preparation Time : 15 minutes

Cooking Time : 30 minutes

Servings : 4

Difficulty Level : Average

Ingredients:

- 1 or 2 large heads cauliflower
- 1/3 cup extra-virgin olive oil
- ¼ teaspoon kosher salt
- 1/8 teaspoon ground black pepper
- Juice of 1 orange
- Zest of 1 orange
- ¼ cup black olives, pitted and chopped
- 1 tablespoon Dijon or grainy mustard
- 1 tablespoon red wine vinegar
- ½ teaspoon ground coriander

Directions:

Preheat the oven to 400°F. Put parchment paper or foil into the baking sheet. Cut off the stem of the cauliflower so it will sit upright. Slice it vertically into four thick slabs. Place the cauliflower on the prepared baking sheet. Dash with the olive oil, salt, and black pepper. Bake for about 30 minutes.

In a medium bowl, stir the orange juice, orange zest, olives, mustard, vinegar, and coriander; mix well. Serve with the sauce.

Nutrition (for 100g): 265 Calories 21g Fat 4g Carbohydrates 5g Protein 693mg Sodium

Pistachio Mint Pesto Pasta

Preparation Time : 10 minutes

Cooking Time : 10 minutes

Servings : 4

Difficulty Level : Average

Ingredients:

- 8 ounces whole-wheat pasta
- 1 cup fresh mint
- ½ cup fresh basil
- 1/3 cup unsalted pistachios, shelled
- 1 garlic clove, peeled
- ½ teaspoon kosher salt
- Juice of ½ lime
- 1/3 cup extra-virgin olive oil

Directions:

Cook the pasta following the package directions. Drain, reserving ½ cup of the pasta water, and set aside. In a food processor, add the mint, basil, pistachios, garlic, salt, and lime juice. Process until the pistachios are coarsely ground. Stir in the olive oil in a slow, steady stream and process until incorporated.

In a large bowl, incorporate the pasta with the pistachio pesto. If a thinner, more saucy consistency is desired, add some of the reserved pasta water and toss well.

Nutrition (for 100g): 420 Calories3g Fat 2g Carbohydrates 11g Protein 593mg Sodium

Burst Cherry Tomato Sauce with Angel Hair Pasta

Preparation Time : 10 minutes

Cooking Time : 20 minutes

Servings : 4

Difficulty Level : Average

Ingredients:

- 8 ounces angel hair pasta
- 2 tablespoons extra-virgin olive oil
- 3 garlic cloves, minced
- 3 pints cherry tomatoes
- ½ teaspoon kosher salt
- ¼ teaspoon red pepper flakes
- ¾ cup fresh basil, chopped
- 1 tablespoon white balsamic vinegar (optional)
- ¼ cup grated Parmesan cheese (optional)

Directions:

Cook the pasta following the package directions. Drain and set aside.

Cook the olive oil in a skillet or large sauté pan over medium-high heat. Stir in the garlic and sauté for 30 seconds. Mix in the tomatoes, salt, and red pepper flakes and cook, stirring occasionally, until the tomatoes burst, about 15 minutes.

Take out from the heat and stir in the pasta and basil. Toss together well. (For out-of-season tomatoes, add the vinegar, if desired, and mix well.) Serve.

Nutrition (for 100g): 305 Calories 8g Fat 3g Carbohydrates 11g Protein 559mg Sodium

Baked Tofu with Sun-Dried Tomatoes and Artichokes

Preparation Time : 30 minutes

Cooking Time : 30 minutes

Servings : 4

Difficulty Level : Average

Ingredients:

- 1 (16-ounce) package extra-firm tofu, cut into 1-inch cubes
- 2 tablespoons extra-virgin olive oil, divided
- 2 tablespoons lemon juice, divided
- 1 tablespoon low-sodium soy sauce
- 1 onion, diced
- ½ teaspoon kosher salt
- 2 garlic cloves, minced
- 1 (14-ounce) can artichoke hearts, drained
- 8 sun-dried tomato
- ¼ teaspoon freshly ground black pepper
- 1 tablespoon white wine vinegar
- Zest of 1 lemon
- ¼ cup fresh parsley, chopped

Directions:

Prepare the oven to 400°F. Position the foil or parchment paper into the baking sheet. In a bowl, combine the tofu, 1 tablespoon of the olive oil, 1 tablespoon of the lemon juice, and the soy sauce. Set aside and marinate for 15 to 30 minutes. Arrange the tofu in a single layer on the prepared baking sheet and bake for 20 minutes, turning once, until light golden brown.

Cook the remaining 1 tablespoon olive oil in a large skillet or sauté pan over medium heat. Add the onion and salt; sauté until translucent, 5 to 6 minutes. Mix in the garlic and sauté for 30 seconds. Then put the artichoke hearts, sun-dried tomatoes, and black pepper and sauté for 5 minutes. Add the white wine vinegar and the remaining 1 tablespoon lemon juice and deglaze the pan, scraping up any brown bits. Take the pan from the heat and put in the lemon zest and parsley. Gently mix in the baked tofu.

Nutrition (for 100g): 230 Calories 14g Fat 5g Carbohydrates 14g Protein 593mg Sodium

Baked Mediterranean Tempeh with Tomatoes and Garlic

Preparation Time : 25 minutes, plus 4 hours to marinate

Cooking Time : 35 minutes

Servings : 4

Difficulty Level : Difficult

Ingredients:

- <u>For the Tempeh</u>
- 12 ounces tempeh
- ¼ cup white wine
- 2 tablespoons extra-virgin olive oil
- 2 tablespoons lemon juice
- Zest of 1 lemon
- ¼ teaspoon kosher salt
- ¼ teaspoon freshly ground black pepper
- <u>For the Tomatoes and Garlic Sauce</u>
- 1 tablespoon extra-virgin olive oil
- 1 onion, diced
- 3 garlic cloves, minced
- 1 (14.5-ounce) can no-salt-added crushed tomatoes
- 1 beefsteak tomato, diced
- 1 dried bay leaf
- 1 teaspoon white wine vinegar

- 1 teaspoon lemon juice
- 1 teaspoon dried oregano
- 1 teaspoon dried thyme
- ¾ teaspoon kosher salt
- ¼ cup basil, cut into ribbons

Directions:

To Make the Tempeh

Place the tempeh in a medium saucepan. Fill enough water to cover it by 1 to 2 inches. Bring to a boil over medium-high heat, cover, and lower heat to a simmer. Cook for 10 to 15 minutes. Remove the tempeh, pat dry, cool, and cut into 1-inch cubes.

Mix the white wine, olive oil, lemon juice, lemon zest, salt, and black pepper. Add the tempeh, cover the bowl, put in the refrigerator for 4 hours, or overnight. Preheat the oven to 375°F. Place the marinated tempeh and the marinade in a baking dish and cook for 15 minutes.

To Make the Tomatoes and Garlic Sauce

Cook the olive oil in a large skillet over medium heat. Add the onion and sauté until transparent, 3 to 5 minutes. Mix in the garlic and sauté for 30 seconds. Add the crushed tomatoes, beefsteak tomato, bay leaf, vinegar, lemon juice, oregano, thyme, and salt. Mix well. Simmer for 15 minutes.

Add the baked tempeh to the tomato mixture and gently mix together. Garnish with the basil.

SUBSTITUTION TIP: If you're out of tempeh or simply want to speed up the cooking process, you can swap in a 14.5-ounce can of white beans for the tempeh. Rinse the beans and put them to the sauce with the crushed tomatoes. It still makes a great vegan entrée in half the time!

Nutrition (for 100g): 330 Calories 20g Fat 4g Carbohydrates 18g Protein 693mg Sodium

Roasted Portobello Mushrooms with Kale and Red Onion

Preparation Time : 30 minutes

Cooking Time : 30 minutes

Servings : 4

Difficulty Level : Difficult

Ingredients:

- ¼ cup white wine vinegar
- 3 tablespoons extra-virgin olive oil, divided
- ½ teaspoon honey
- ¾ teaspoon kosher salt, divided
- ¼ teaspoon freshly ground black pepper
- 4 large portobello mushrooms, stems removed
- 1 red onion, julienned
- 2 garlic cloves, minced
- 1 (8-ounce) bunch kale, stemmed and chopped small
- ¼ teaspoon red pepper flakes
- ¼ cup grated Parmesan or Romano cheese

Directions:

Situate parchment paper or foil into the baking sheet. In a medium bowl, whisk together the vinegar, 1½ tablespoons of the olive oil, honey, ¼ teaspoon of the salt, and the black pepper. Lay the mushrooms on the baking sheet and pour the marinade over them. Marinate for 15 to 30 minutes.

Meanwhile, preheat the oven to 400°F. Bake the mushrooms for 20 minutes, turning over halfway through. Heat the remaining 1½ tablespoons olive oil in a large skillet or ovenproof sauté pan over medium-high heat. Add the onion and the remaining ½ teaspoon salt and sauté until golden brown, 5 to 6 minutes. Mix in the garlic and sauté for 30 seconds. Mix in the kale and red pepper flakes and sauté until the kale cooks down, about 5 minutes.

Remove the mushrooms from the oven and increase the temperature to broil. Carefully pour the liquid from the baking sheet into the pan with the kale mixture; mix well. Turn the mushrooms over so that the stem side is facing up. Spoon some of the kale mixture on top of each mushroom. Sprinkle 1 tablespoon Parmesan cheese on top of each. Broil until golden brown.

Nutrition (For 100g): 200 Calories 13g Fat 4g Carbohydrates 8g Protein

Balsamic Marinated Tofu with Basil and Oregano

Preparation Time : 40 minutes

Cooking Time : 30 minutes

Servings : 4

Difficulty Level : Average

Ingredients:

- ¼ cup extra-virgin olive oil
- ¼ cup balsamic vinegar
- 2 tablespoons low-sodium soy sauce
- 3 garlic cloves, grated
- 2 teaspoons pure maple syrup
- Zest of 1 lemon
- 1 teaspoon dried basil
- 1 teaspoon dried oregano
- ½ teaspoon dried thyme
- ½ teaspoon dried sage
- ¼ teaspoon kosher salt
- ¼ teaspoon freshly ground black pepper
- ¼ teaspoon red pepper flakes (optional)
- 1 (16-ounce) block extra firm tofu

Directions:

In a bowl or gallon zip-top bag, mix together the olive oil, vinegar, soy sauce, garlic, maple syrup, lemon zest, basil, oregano, thyme, sage, salt, black pepper, and red pepper flakes, if desired. Add the tofu and mix gently. Put in the refrigerator and marinate for 30 minutes, or up to overnight if you desire.

Prepare the oven to 425°F. Place parchment paper or foil into the baking sheet. Arrange the marinated tofu in a single layer on the prepared baking sheet. Bake for 20 to 30 minutes, flip over halfway through, until slightly crispy.

Nutrition (for 100g): 225 Calories 16g Fat 2g Carbohydrates 13g Protein 493mg Sodium

Ricotta, Basil, and Pistachio–Stuffed Zucchini

Preparation Time : 15 minutes

Cooking Time : 25 minutes

Servings : 4

Difficulty Level : Average

Ingredients:

- 2 medium zucchinis, halved lengthwise
- 1 tablespoon extra-virgin olive oil
- 1 onion, diced
- 1 teaspoon kosher salt
- 2 garlic cloves, minced
- ¾ cup ricotta cheese
- ¼ cup unsalted pistachios, shelled and chopped
- ¼ cup fresh basil, chopped
- 1 large egg, beaten
- ¼ teaspoon freshly ground black pepper

Directions:

Ready the oven to 425°F. Situate parchment paper or foil into the baking sheet. Scoop out the seeds/pulp from the zucchini, leaving ¼-inch flesh around the edges. Situate the pulp to a cutting board and chop off the pulp.

Cook the olive oil in a sauté pan over medium heat. Add the onion, pulp, and salt and sauté about 5 minutes. Add the garlic and sauté 30 seconds. Mix the ricotta cheese, pistachios, basil, egg, and black pepper. Add the onion mixture and mix well.

Place the 4 zucchini halves on the prepared baking sheet. Spread the zucchini halves with the ricotta mixture. Bake until golden brown.

Nutrition (for 100g): 200 Calories 12g Fat 3g Carbohydrates 11g Protein 836mg Sodium

Farro with Roasted Tomatoes and Mushrooms

Preparation Time : 20 minutes

Cooking Time : 1 hour

Servings : 4

Difficulty Level : Difficult

Ingredients:

- <u>For the Tomatoes</u>
- 2 pints cherry tomatoes
- 1 teaspoon extra-virgin olive oil
- ¼ teaspoon kosher salt
- <u>For the Farro</u>
- 3 to 4 cups water
- ½ cup farro
- ¼ teaspoon kosher salt
- <u>For the Mushrooms</u>
- 2 tablespoons extra-virgin olive oil
- 1 onion, julienned
- ½ teaspoon kosher salt
- ¼ teaspoon freshly ground black pepper
- 10 ounces baby bell mushrooms, stemmed and sliced thin
- ½ cup no-salt-added vegetable stock

- 1 (15-ounce) can low-sodium cannellini beans, drained and rinsed
- 1 cup baby spinach
- 2 tablespoons fresh basil, cut into ribbons
- ¼ cup pine nuts, toasted
- Aged balsamic vinegar (optional)

Directions:

To Make the Tomatoes

Preheat the oven to 400°F. Put parchment paper or foil into the baking sheet. Mix the tomatoes, olive oil, and salt together on the baking sheet and roast for 30 minutes.

To Make the Farro

Bring the water, farro, and salt to a boil in a medium saucepan or pot over high heat. Allow to simmer, and cook for 30 minutes, or until the farro is al dente. Drain and set aside.

To Make the Mushrooms

Cook the olive oil in a large skillet or sauté pan over medium-low heat. Add the onions, salt, and black pepper and sauté until golden brown and starting to caramelize, about 15 minutes. Stir in the mushrooms, increase the heat to medium, and sauté until the liquid has evaporated and the mushrooms brown, about 10 minutes. Stir in the vegetable stock and deglaze the pan, scraping up any brown bits, and reduce the liquid for about 5 minutes. Add the beans and warm through, about 3 minutes.

Remove and stir in the spinach, basil, pine nuts, roasted tomatoes, and farro. Dash with balsamic vinegar, if desired.

Nutrition (for 100g): 375 Calories 15g Fat 10g Carbohydrates 14g Protein 769mg Sodium

Baked Orzo with Eggplant, Swiss Chard, and Mozzarella

Preparation Time : 20 minutes

Cooking Time : 60 minutes

Servings : 4

Difficulty Level : Average

Ingredients:

- 2 tablespoons extra-virgin olive oil
- 1 large (1-pound) eggplant, diced small
- 2 carrots, peeled and diced small
- 2 celery stalks, diced small
- 1 onion, diced small
- ½ teaspoon kosher salt
- 3 garlic cloves, minced
- ¼ teaspoon freshly ground black pepper
- 1 cup whole-wheat orzo
- 1 teaspoon no-salt-added tomato paste
- 1½ cups no-salt-added vegetable stock
- 1 cup Swiss chard, stemmed and chopped small
- 2 tablespoons fresh oregano, chopped
- Zest of 1 lemon
- 4 ounces mozzarella cheese, diced small
- ¼ cup grated Parmesan cheese
- 2 tomatoes, sliced ½-inch-thick

Directions:

Preheat the oven to 400°F. Cook the olive oil in a large oven-safe sauté pan over medium heat. Add the eggplant, carrots, celery, onion, and salt and sauté about 10 minutes. Add the garlic and black pepper and sauté about 30 seconds. Add the orzo and tomato paste and sauté 1 minute. Mix in the vegetable stock and deglaze the pan, scraping up the brown bits. Add the Swiss chard, oregano, and lemon zest and stir until the chard wilts.

Pull out and put in the mozzarella cheese. Smooth the top of the orzo mixture flat. Sprinkle the Parmesan cheese over the top. Spread the tomatoes in a single layer on top of the Parmesan cheese. Bake for 45 minutes.

Nutrition (for 100g): 470 Calories 17g Fat 7g Carbohydrates 18g Protein 769mg Sodium

Barley Risotto with Tomatoes

Preparation Time : 20 minutes

Cooking Time : 45 minutes

Servings : 4

Difficulty Level : Average

Ingredients:

- 2 tablespoons extra-virgin olive oil
- 2 celery stalks, diced
- ½ cup shallots, diced
- 4 garlic cloves, minced
- 3 cups no-salt-added vegetable stock
- 1 (14.5-ounce) can no-salt-added diced tomatoes
- 1 (14.5-ounce) can no-salt-added crushed tomatoes
- 1 cup pearl barley
- Zest of 1 lemon
- 1 teaspoon kosher salt
- ½ teaspoon smoked paprika
- ¼ teaspoon red pepper flakes
- ¼ teaspoon freshly ground black pepper
- 4 thyme sprigs
- 1 dried bay leaf
- 2 cups baby spinach
- ½ cup crumbled feta cheese
- 1 tablespoon fresh oregano, chopped

- 1 tablespoon fennel seeds, toasted (optional)

Directions:

Cook the olive oil in a large saucepan over medium heat. Add the celery and shallots and sauté, about 4 to 5 minutes. Add the garlic and sauté 30 seconds. Add the vegetable stock, diced tomatoes, crushed tomatoes, barley, lemon zest, salt, paprika, red pepper flakes, black pepper, thyme, and the bay leaf, and mix well. Let it boil, then lower to low, and simmer. Cook, stirring occasionally, for 40 minutes.

Remove the bay leaf and thyme sprigs. Stir in the spinach. In a small bowl, combine the feta, oregano, and fennel seeds. Serve the barley risotto in bowls topped with the feta mixture.

Nutrition (for 100g): 375 Calories 12g Fat 13g Carbohydrates 11g Protein 799mg Sodium

Chickpeas and Kale with Spicy Pomodoro Sauce

Preparation Time : 10 minutes

Cooking Time : 35 minutes

Servings : 4

Difficulty Level : Easy

Ingredients:

- 2 tablespoons extra-virgin olive oil
- 4 garlic cloves, sliced
- 1 teaspoon red pepper flakes
- 1 (28-ounce) can no-salt-added crushed tomatoes
- 1 teaspoon kosher salt
- ½ teaspoon honey
- 1 bunch kale, stemmed and chopped
- 2 (15-ounce) cans low-sodium chickpeas, drained and rinsed
- ¼ cup fresh basil, chopped
- ¼ cup grated pecorino Romano cheese

Directions:

Cook the olive oil in a sauté pan over medium heat. Stir in the garlic and red pepper flakes and sauté until the garlic is a light golden brown, about 2 minutes. Add the tomatoes, salt, and honey and mix well. Reduce the heat to low and simmer for 20 minutes.

Add the kale and mix in well. Cook about 5 minutes. Add the chickpeas and simmer about 5 minutes. Remove from heat and stir in the basil. Serve topped with pecorino cheese.

Nutrition (for 100g): 420 Calories 13g Fat 12g Carbohydrates 20g Protein 882mg Sodium

Roasted Feta with Kale and Lemon Yogurt

Preparation Time : 15 minutes

Cooking Time : 20 minutes

Servings : 4

Difficulty Level : Average

Ingredients:

- 1 tablespoon extra-virgin olive oil
- 1 onion, julienned
- ¼ teaspoon kosher salt
- 1 teaspoon ground turmeric
- ½ teaspoon ground cumin
- ½ teaspoon ground coriander
- ¼ teaspoon freshly ground black pepper
- 1 bunch kale, stemmed and chopped
- 7-ounce block feta cheese, cut into ¼-inch-thick slices
- ½ cup plain Greek yogurt
- 1 tablespoon lemon juice

Directions:

Preheat the oven to 400°F. Fry the olive oil in a large ovenproof skillet or sauté pan over medium heat. Add the onion and salt; sauté until lightly golden brown, about 5 minutes. Add the turmeric, cumin, coriander, and black pepper; sauté for 30 seconds. Add the kale and sauté about 2 minutes. Add ½ cup water and continue to cook down the kale, about 3 minutes.

Remove from the heat and place the feta cheese slices on top of the kale mixture. Introduce in the oven and bake until the feta softens, 10 to 12 minutes. In a small bowl, combine the yogurt and lemon juice. Serve the kale and feta cheese topped with the lemon yogurt.

Nutrition (for 100g): 210 Calories 14g Fat 2g Carbohydrates 11g Protein 836mg Sodium

Roasted Eggplant and Chickpeas with Tomato Sauce

Preparation Time : 15 minutes

Cooking Time : 60 minutes

Servings : 4

Difficulty Level : Difficult

Ingredients:

- Olive oil cooking spray
- 1 large (about 1 pound) eggplant, sliced into ¼-inch-thick rounds
- 1 teaspoon kosher salt, divided
- 1 tablespoon extra-virgin olive oil
- 3 garlic cloves, minced
- 1 (28-ounce) can no-salt-added crushed tomatoes
- ½ teaspoon honey
- ¼ teaspoon freshly ground black pepper
- 2 tablespoons fresh basil, chopped
- 1 (15-ounce) can no-salt-added or low-sodium chickpeas, drained and rinsed
- ¾ cup crumbled feta cheese
- 1 tablespoon fresh oregano, chopped

Directions:

Preheat the oven to 425°F. Grease and line two baking sheets with foil and lightly spray with olive oil cooking spray. Spread the eggplant in a single layer and sprinkle with ½ teaspoon of the salt. Bake for 20 minutes, turning once halfway, until lightly golden brown.

Meanwhile, heat the olive oil in a large saucepan over medium heat. Mix in the garlic and sauté for 30 seconds. Add the crushed tomatoes, honey, the remaining ½ teaspoon salt, and black pepper. Simmer about 20 minutes, until the sauce reduces a bit and thickens. Stir in the basil.

After removing the eggplant from the oven, reduce the oven temperature to 375°F. In a large rectangular or oval baking dish, spoon in the chickpeas and 1 cup sauce. Layer the eggplant slices on top, overlapping as necessary to cover the chickpeas. Lay the remaining sauce on top of the eggplant. Sprinkle the feta cheese and oregano on top.

Wrap the baking dish with foil and bake for 15 minutes. Pull out the foil and bake an additional 15 minutes.

Nutrition (for 100g): 320 Calories 11g Fat 12g Carbohydrates 14g Protein 773mg Sodium

Baked Falafel Sliders

Preparation Time : 10 minutes

Cooking Time : 30 minutes

Servings : 6

Difficulty Level : Average

Ingredients:

- Olive oil cooking spray
- 1 (15-ounce) can low-sodium chickpeas, drained and rinsed
- 1 onion, roughly chopped
- 2 garlic cloves, peeled
- 2 tablespoons fresh parsley, chopped
- 2 tablespoons whole-wheat flour
- ½ teaspoon ground coriander
- ½ teaspoon ground cumin
- ½ teaspoon baking powder
- ½ teaspoon kosher salt
- ¼ teaspoon freshly ground black pepper

Directions:

Preheat the oven to 350°F. Put parchment paper or foil and lightly spray with olive oil cooking spray in the baking sheet.

In a food processor, mix in the chickpeas, onion, garlic, parsley, flour, coriander, cumin, baking powder, salt, and black pepper. Blend until smooth.

Make 6 slider patties, each with a heaping ¼ cup of mixture, and arrange on the prepared baking sheet. Bake for 30 minutes. Serve.

Nutrition (for 100g): 90 Calories 1g Fat 3g Carbohydrates 4g Protein 803mg Sodium

Portobello Caprese

Preparation Time : 15 minutes

Cooking Time : 30 minutes

Servings : 2

Difficulty Level : Difficult

Ingredients:

- 1 tablespoon olive oil
- 1 cup cherry tomatoes
- Salt and black pepper, to taste
- 4 large fresh basil leaves, thinly sliced, divided
- 3 medium garlic cloves, minced
- 2 large portobello mushrooms, stems removed
- 4 pieces mini Mozzarella balls
- 1 tablespoon Parmesan cheese, grated

Directions:

Prepare the oven to 350°F (180ºC). Grease a baking pan with olive oil. Drizzle 1 tablespoon olive oil in a nonstick skillet, and heat over medium-high heat. Add the tomatoes to the skillet, and sprinkle salt and black pepper to season. Prick some holes on the tomatoes for juice during the cooking. Put the lid on and cook the tomatoes for 10 minutes or until tender.

Reserve 2 teaspoons of basil and add the remaining basil and garlic to the skillet. Crush the tomatoes with a spatula, then cook for half a minute. Stir constantly during the cooking. Set aside. Arrange the mushrooms in the baking pan, cap side down, and sprinkle with salt and black pepper to taste.

Spoon the tomato mixture and Mozzarella balls on the gill of the mushrooms, then scatter with Parmesan cheese to coat well. Bake until the mushrooms are fork-tender and the cheeses are browned. Pull out the stuffed mushrooms from the oven and serve with basil on top.

Nutrition (for 100g): 285 Calories 21.8g Fat 2.1g Carbohydrates 14.3g Protein 823mg Sodium

Mushroom and Cheese Stuffed Tomatoes

Preparation Time : 15 minutes

Cooking Time : 20 minutes

Servings : 4

Difficulty Level : Average

Ingredients:

- 4 large ripe tomatoes
- 1 tablespoon olive oil
- ½ pound (454 g) white or cremini mushrooms, sliced
- 1 tablespoon fresh basil, chopped
- ½ cup yellow onion, diced
- 1 tablespoon fresh oregano, chopped
- 2 garlic cloves, minced
- ½ teaspoon salt
- ¼ teaspoon freshly ground black pepper
- 1 cup part-skim Mozzarella cheese, shredded
- 1 tablespoon Parmesan cheese, grated

Directions:

Ready the oven to 375°F (190ºC). Cut a ½-inch slice off the top of each tomato. Scoop the pulp into a bowl and leave ½-inch tomato shells. Arrange the tomatoes on a baking sheet lined with aluminum foil. Heat the olive oil in a nonstick skillet over medium heat.

Add the mushrooms, basil, onion, oregano, garlic, salt, and black pepper to the skillet and sauté for 5 minutes.

Pour the mixture to the tomato pulp bowl, then add the Mozzarella cheese and stir to combine well. Spoon the mixture into each tomato shell, then top with a layer of Parmesan. Bake in the preheated oven for 15 minutes or until the cheese is bubbly and the tomatoes are soft. Pull out the stuffed tomatoes from the oven and serve warm.

Nutrition (for 100g): 254 Calories 14.7g Fat 5.2g Carbohydrates 17.5g Protein 783mg Sodium

Tabbouleh

Preparation Time : 15 minutes

Cooking Time : 5 minutes

Servings : 6

Difficulty Level : Average

Ingredients:

- 4 tablespoons olive oil, divided
- 4 cups riced cauliflower
- 3 garlic cloves, finely minced
- Salt and black pepper, to taste
- ½ large cucumber, peeled, seeded, and chopped
- ½ cup Italian parsley, chopped
- Juice of 1 lemon
- 2 tablespoons minced red onion
- ½ cup mint leaves, chopped
- ½ cup pitted Kalamata olives, chopped
- 1 cup cherry tomatoes, quartered
- 2 cups baby arugula or spinach leaves
- 2 medium avocados, peeled, pitted, and diced

Directions:

Warm 2 tablespoons olive oil in a nonstick skillet over medium-high heat. Add the rice cauliflower, garlic, salt, and black pepper to the skillet and sauté for 3 minutes or until fragrant. Transfer them to a large bowl.

Add the cucumber, parsley, lemon juice, red onion, mint, olives, and remaining olive oil to the bowl. Toss to combine well. Reserve the bowl in the refrigerator for at least 30 minutes.

Remove the bowl from the refrigerator. Add the cherry tomatoes, arugula, avocado to the bowl. Season well, and toss to combine well. Serve chilled.

Nutrition (for 100g): 198 Calories 17.5g Fat 6.2g Carbohydrates 4.2g Protein 773mg Sodium

Spicy Broccoli Rabe And Artichoke Hearts

Preparation Time : 5 minutes

Cooking Time : 15 minutes

Servings : 4

Difficulty Level : Average

Ingredients:

- 3 tablespoons olive oil, divided
- 2 pounds (907 g) fresh broccoli rabe
- 3 garlic cloves, finely minced
- 1 teaspoon red pepper flakes
- 1 teaspoon salt, plus more to taste
- 13.5 ounces (383 g) artichoke hearts
- 1 tablespoon water
- 2 tablespoons red wine vinegar
- Freshly ground black pepper, to taste

Directions:

Warm 2 tablespoons olive oil in a nonstick skillet over medium-high skillet. Add the broccoli, garlic, red pepper flakes, and salt to the skillet and sauté for 5 minutes or until the broccoli is soft.

Put the artichoke hearts to the skillet and sauté for 2 more minutes or until tender. Add water to the skillet and turn down the heat to low. Put the lid on and simmer for 5 minutes. Meanwhile, combine the vinegar and 1 tablespoon of olive oil in a bowl.

Drizzle the simmered broccoli and artichokes with oiled vinegar, and sprinkle with salt and black pepper. Toss to combine well before serving.

Nutrition (for 100g): 272 Calories 21.5g Fat 9.8g Carbohydrates 11.2g Protein 736mg Sodium

Shakshuka

Preparation Time : 10 minutes

Cooking Time : 25 minutes

Servings : 4

Difficulty Level : Difficult

Ingredients:

- 5 tablespoons olive oil, divided
- 1 red bell pepper, finely diced
- ½ small yellow onion, finely diced
- 14 ounces (397 g) crushed tomatoes, with juices
- 6 ounces (170 g) frozen spinach, thawed and drained of excess liquid
- 1 teaspoon smoked paprika
- 2 garlic cloves, finely minced
- 2 teaspoons red pepper flakes
- 1 tablespoon capers, roughly chopped
- 1 tablespoon water
- 6 large eggs
- ¼ teaspoon freshly ground black pepper
- ¾ cup feta or goat cheese, crumbled
- ¼ cup fresh flat-leaf parsley or cilantro, chopped

Directions:

Ready the oven to 300ºF (150ºC). Heat 2 tablespoons olive oil in an oven-safe skillet over medium-high heat. Sauté the bell pepper and onion to the skillet until the onion is translucent and the bell pepper is soft.

Add the tomatoes and juices, spinach, paprika, garlic, red pepper flakes, capers, water, and 2 tablespoons olive oil to the skillet. Stir well and bring to a boil. Set down the heat to low, then put the lid on and simmer for 5 minutes.

Crack the eggs over the sauce, keep a little space between each egg, leave the egg intact and sprinkle with freshly ground black pepper. Cook until the eggs reach the right doneness.

Scatter the cheese over the eggs and sauce, and bake in the preheated oven for 5 minutes or until the cheese is frothy and golden brown. Drizzle with the remaining 1 tablespoon olive oil and spread the parsley on top before serving warm.

Nutrition (for 100g): 335 Calories 26.5g Fat 5g Carbohydrates 16.8g Protein 736mg Sodium

Spanakopita

Preparation Time : 15 minutes

Cooking Time : 50 minutes

Servings : 6

Difficulty Level : Difficult

Ingredients:

- 6 tablespoons olive oil, divided
- 1 small yellow onion, diced
- 4 cups frozen chopped spinach
- 4 garlic cloves, minced
- ½ teaspoon salt
- ½ teaspoon freshly ground black pepper
- 4 large eggs, beaten
- 1 cup ricotta cheese
- ¾ cup feta cheese, crumbled
- ¼ cup pine nuts

Directions:

Grease baking dish with 2 tablespoons olive oil. Organize the oven at 375 degrees F. Heat 2 tablespoons olive oil in a nonstick skillet over medium-high heat. Mix in the onion to the skillet and sauté for 6 minutes or until translucent and tender.

Add the spinach, garlic, salt, and black pepper to the skillet and sauté for 5 minutes more. Place them to a bowl and set aside.

Combine the beaten eggs and ricotta cheese in a separate bowl, then pour them in to the bowl of spinach mixture. Stir to mix well.

Fill the mixture into the baking dish, and tilt the dish so the mixture coats the bottom evenly. Bake until it begins to set. Take out the baking dish from the oven, and spread the feta cheese and pine nuts on top, then dash with remaining 2 tablespoons olive oil.

Return the baking dish to the oven and bake for another 15 minutes or until the top is golden brown. Remove the dish from the oven. Allow the spanakopita to cool for a few minutes and slice to serve.

Nutrition (for 100g): 340 Calories 27.3g Fat 10.1g Carbohydrates 18.2g Protein 781mg Sodium

Tagine

Preparation Time : 20 minutes

Cooking Time : 60 minutes

Servings : 6

Difficulty Level : Average

Ingredients:

- ½ cup olive oil
- 6 celery stalks, sliced into ¼-inch crescents
- 2 medium yellow onions, sliced
- 1 teaspoon ground cumin
- ½ teaspoon ground cinnamon
- 1 teaspoon ginger powder
- 6 garlic cloves, minced
- ½ teaspoon paprika
- 1 teaspoon salt
- ¼ teaspoon freshly ground black pepper
- 2 cups low-sodium vegetable stock
- 2 medium zucchinis, cut into ½-inch-thick semicircles
- 2 cups cauliflower, cut into florets
- 1 medium eggplant, cut into 1-inch cubes
- 1 cup green olives, halved and pitted
- 13.5 ounces (383 g) artichoke hearts, drained and quartered
- ½ cup chopped fresh cilantro leaves, for garnish
- ½ cup plain Greek yogurt, for garnish

- ½ cup chopped fresh flat-leaf parsley, for garnish

Directions:

Cook the olive oil in a stockpot over medium-high heat. Add the celery and onion to the pot and sauté for 6 minutes. Put the cumin, cinnamon, ginger, garlic, paprika, salt, and black pepper to the pot and sauté for 2 minutes more until aromatic.

Pour the vegetable stock to the pot and bring to a boil. Turn down the heat to low, and add the zucchini, cauliflower, and eggplant to the bank. Cover and simmer for 30 minutes or until the vegetables are soft. Then add the olives and artichoke hearts to the pool and simmer for 15 minutes more. Fill them into a large serving bowl or a Tagine, then serve with cilantro, Greek yogurt, and parsley on top.

Nutrition (for 100g): 312 Calories 21.2g Fat 9.2g Carbohydrates 6.1g Protein 813mg Sodium

Citrus Pistachios and Asparagus

Preparation Time : 10 minutes

Cooking Time : 10 minutes

Servings : 4

Difficulty Level : Difficult

Ingredients:

- Zest and juice of 2 clementine or 1 orange
- Zest and juice of 1 lemon
- 1 tablespoon red wine vinegar
- 3 tablespoons extra-virgin olive oil, divided
- 1 teaspoon salt, divided
- ¼ teaspoon freshly ground black pepper
- ½ cup pistachios, shelled
- 1 pound (454 g) fresh asparagus, trimmed
- 1 tablespoon water

Directions:

Combine the zest and juice of clementine and lemon, vinegar, 2 tablespoons of olive oil, ½ teaspoon of salt, and black pepper. Stir to mix well. Set aside.

Toast the pistachios in a nonstick skillet over medium-high heat for 2 minutes or until golden brown. Transfer the roasted pistachios to a clean work surface, then chop roughly. Mix the pistachios with the citrus mixture. Set aside.

Heat the remaining olive oil in the nonstick skillet over medium-high heat. Add the asparagus to the skillet and sauté for 2 minutes, then season with remaining salt. Add the water to the skillet. Put down the heat to low, and put the lid on. Simmer for 4 minutes until the asparagus is tender.

Remove the asparagus from the skillet to a large dish. Pour the citrus and pistachios mixture over the asparagus. Toss to coat well before serving.

Nutrition (for 100g): 211 Calories 17.5g Fat 3.8g Carbohydrates 5.9g Protein 901mg Sodium

Tomato and Parsley Stuffed Eggplant

Preparation Time : 15 minutes

Cooking Time : 2 hours and 10 minutes

Servings : 6

Difficulty Level : Average

Ingredients:

- ¼ cup extra-virgin olive oil

- 3 small eggplants, cut in half lengthwise

- 1 teaspoon sea salt

- ½ teaspoon freshly ground black pepper

- 1 large yellow onion, finely chopped

- 4 garlic cloves, minced

- 15 ounces (425 g) diced tomatoes, with the juice

- ¼ cup fresh flat-leaf parsley, finely chopped

Directions:

Put the insert of the slow cooker with 2 tablespoons of olive oil. Cut some slits on the cut side of each eggplant half, keep a ¼-inch space between each slit. Place the eggplant halves in the slow cooker, skin side down. Sprinkle with salt and black pepper.

Warm up the remaining olive oil in a nonstick skillet over medium-high heat. Add the onion and garlic to the skillet and sauté for 3 minutes or until the onion is translucent.

Add the parsley and tomatoes with the juice to the skillet, and sprinkle with salt and black pepper. Sauté for 5 more minutes or until they are tender. Divide and spoon the mixture in the skillet on the eggplant halves.

Situate the slow cooker lid on and cook on HIGH for 2 hours until the eggplant is soft. Transfer the eggplant to a plate, and allow to cool for a few minutes before serving.

Nutrition (for 100g): 455 Calories 13g Fat 14g Carbohydrates 14g Protein 719mg Sodium

Ratatouille

Preparation Time : 15 minutes

Cooking Time : 7 hours

Servings : 6

Difficulty Level : Average

Ingredients:

- 3 tablespoons extra-virgin olive oil
- 1 large eggplant, unpeeled, sliced
- 2 large onions, sliced
- 4 small zucchinis, sliced
- 2 green bell peppers
- 6 large tomatoes, cut in ½-inch wedges
- 2 tablespoons fresh flat-leaf parsley, chopped
- 1 teaspoon dried basil
- 2 garlic cloves, minced
- 2 teaspoons sea salt
- ¼ teaspoon freshly ground black pepper

Direction:

Fill the insert of the slow cooker with 2 tablespoons olive oil. Arrange the vegetables slices, strips, and wedges alternately in the insert of the slow cooker. Spread the parsley on top of the vegetables, and season with basil, garlic, salt, and black pepper. Drizzle with the remaining olive oil. Close and cook on LOW for 7 hours until the vegetables are tender. Transfer the vegetables on a plate and serve warm.

Nutrition (for 100g): 265 Calories 1.7g Fat 13.7g Carbohydrates 8.3g Protein 800mg Sodium

Gemista

Preparation Time : 15 minutes

Cooking Time : 4 hours

Servings : 4

Difficulty Level : Average

Ingredients:

- 2 tablespoons extra-virgin olive oil
- 4 large bell peppers, any color
- ½ cup uncooked couscous
- 1 teaspoon oregano
- 1 garlic clove, minced
- 1 cup crumbled feta cheese
- 1 (15-ounce / 425-g) can cannellini beans, rinsed and drained
- Salt and pepper, to taste
- 1 lemon wedges
- 4 green onions, white and green parts separated, thinly sliced

Direction:

Cut a ½-inch slice below the stem from the top of the bell pepper. Discard the stem only and chop the sliced top portion under the stem, and reserve in a bowl. Hollow the bell pepper with a spoon. Grease the slow cooker with oil.

Incorporate the remaining ingredients, except for the green parts of the green onion and lemon wedges, to the bowl of chopped bell pepper top. Stir to mix well. Spoon the mixture in the hollowed bell pepper, and arrange the stuffed bell peppers in the slow cooker, then drizzle with more olive oil.

Seal the slow cooker lid on and cook on HIGH for 4 hours or until the bell peppers are soft.

Remove the bell peppers from the slow cooker and serve on a plate. Sprinkle with green parts of the green onions, and squeeze the lemon wedges on top before serving.

Nutrition (for 100g): 246 Calories 9g Fat 6.5g Carbohydrates 11.1g Protein 698mg Sodium

Stuffed Cabbage Rolls

Preparation Time : 15 minutes

Cooking Time : 2 hours

Servings : 4

Difficulty Level : Difficult

Ingredients:

- 4 tablespoons olive oil, divided
- 1 large head green cabbage, cored
- 1 large yellow onion, chopped
- 3 ounces (85 g) feta cheese, crumbled
- ½ cup dried currants
- 3 cups cooked pearl barley
- 2 tablespoons fresh flat-leaf parsley, chopped
- 2 tablespoons pine nuts, toasted
- ½ teaspoon sea salt
- ½ teaspoon black pepper
- 15 ounces (425 g) crushed tomatoes, with the juice
- 1 tablespoon apple cider vinegar
- ½ cup apple juice

Directions:

Brush off the insert of the slow cooker with 2 tablespoons olive oil. Blanch the cabbage in a pot of water for 8 minutes. Take it from the water, and set aside, then separate 16 leaves from the cabbage. Set aside.

Drizzle the remaining olive oil in a nonstick skillet, and heat over medium heat. Stir in the onion to the skillet and cook until the onion and bell pepper is tender. Transfer the onion to a bowl.

Add the feta cheese, currants, barley, parsley, and pine nuts to the bowl of cooked onion, then sprinkle with ¼ teaspoon of salt and ¼ teaspoon of black pepper.

Arrange the cabbage leaves on a clean work surface. Scoop 1/3 cup of the mixture on the center of each plate, then fold the edge onto the mixture and roll it up. Place the cabbage rolls in the slow cooker, seam side down.

Incorporate the remaining ingredients in a separate bowl, then pour the mixture over the cabbage rolls. Seal slow cooker lid on and cook on HIGH for 2 hours. Remove the cabbage rolls from the slow cooker and serve warm.

Nutrition (for 100g): 383 Calories 14.7g Fat 12.9g Carbohydrates 10.7g Protein 838mg Sodium

Brussels Sprouts with Balsamic Glaze

Preparation Time : 15 minutes

Cooking Time : 2 hours

Servings : 6

Difficulty Level : Average

Ingredients:

- Balsamic Glaze:
- 1 cup balsamic vinegar
- ¼ cup honey
- 2 tablespoons extra-virgin olive oil
- 2 pounds (907 g) Brussels sprouts, trimmed and halved
- 2 cups low-sodium vegetable soup
- 1 teaspoon sea salt
- Freshly ground black pepper, to taste
- ¼ cup Parmesan cheese, grated
- ¼ cup pine nuts

Directions:

Make the balsamic glaze: Combine the balsamic vinegar and honey in a saucepan. Stir to mix well. Over medium-high heat, bring to a boil. Set down the heat to low, then simmer for 20 minutes or until the glaze reduces in half and has a thick consistency. Impose some olive oil inside the insert of the slow cooker.

Put the Brussels sprouts, vegetable soup, and ½ teaspoon of salt in the slow cooker, stir to combine. Seal the slow cooker lid on and cook on HIGH for 2 hours until the Brussels sprouts are soft.

Put the Brussels sprouts to a plate, and sprinkle the remaining salt and black pepper to season. Dash the balsamic glaze over the Brussels sprouts, then serve with Parmesan and pine nuts.

Nutrition (for 100g): 270 Calories 10.6g Fat 6.9g Carbohydrates 8.7g Protein 693mg Sodium

Spinach Salad with Citrus Vinaigrette

Preparation Time : 10 minutes

Cooking Time : 0 minutes

Servings : 4

Difficulty Level : Easy

Ingredients:

- Citrus Vinaigrette:
- ¼ cup extra-virgin olive oil
- 3 tablespoons balsamic vinegar
- ½ teaspoon fresh lemon zest
- ½ teaspoon salt
- Salad:
- 1-pound (454 g) baby spinach, washed, stems removed
- 1 large ripe tomato, cut into ¼-inch pieces
- 1 medium red onion, thinly sliced

Directions:

Make the citrus vinaigrette: Stir together the olive oil, balsamic vinegar, lemon zest, and salt in a bowl until mixed well.

Make the salad: Place the baby spinach, tomato and onions in a separate salad bowl. Fill the citrus vinaigrette over the salad and gently toss until the vegetables are coated thoroughly.

Nutrition (for 100g): 173 Calories 14.2g Fat 4.2g Carbohydrates 4.1g Protein 699mg Sodium

Simple Celery and Orange Salad

Preparation Time : 15 minutes

Cooking Time : 0 minutes

Servings : 6

Difficulty Level : Easy

Ingredients:

- Salad:
- 3 celery stalks, including leaves, sliced diagonally into ½-inch slices
- ½ cup green olives
- ¼ cup sliced red onion
- 2 large peeled oranges, cut into rounds
- Dressing:
- 1 tablespoon extra-virgin olive oil
- 1 tablespoon lemon or orange juice
- 1 tablespoon olive brine
- ¼ teaspoon kosher or sea salt
- ¼ teaspoon freshly ground black pepper

Directions:

Make the salad: Put the celery stalks, green olives, onion, and oranges in a shallow bowl. Mix well and set aside.

Make the dressing: Stir the olive oil, lemon juice, olive brine, salt, and pepper well.

Fill the dressing into the bowl of salad and lightly toss until coated thoroughly.

Serve chilled or at room temperature.

Nutrition (for 100g): 24 Calories 1.2g Fat 1.2g Carbohydrates 1.1g Protein 813mg Sodium

Fried Eggplant Rolls

Preparation Time : 20 minutes

Cooking Time : 10 minutes

Servings : 6

Difficulty Level : Average

Ingredients:

- 2 large eggplants
- 1 teaspoon salt
- 1 cup shredded ricotta cheese
- 4 ounces (113 g) goat cheese, shredded
- ¼ cup finely chopped fresh basil
- ½ teaspoon freshly ground black pepper
- Olive oil spray

Directions:

Add the eggplant slices to a colander and season with salt. Set aside for 15 to 20 minutes.

Mix together the ricotta and goat cheese, basil, and black pepper in a large bowl and stir to combine. Set aside. Pat dry the eggplant slices with paper towels and lightly mist them with olive oil spray.

Warm up large skillet over medium heat and lightly spray it with olive oil spray. Arrange the eggplant slices in the skillet and fry each side for 3 minutes until golden brown.

Remove from the heat to a paper towel-lined plate and rest for 5 minutes. Make the eggplant rolls: Lay the eggplant slices on a flat work surface and top each slice with a tablespoon of the prepared cheese mixture. Roll them up and serve immediately.

Nutrition (for 100g): 254 Calories 14.9g Fat 7.1g Carbohydrates 15.3g Protein 612mg Sodium

Roasted Veggies and Brown Rice Bowl

Preparation Time : 15 minutes

Cooking Time : 20 minutes

Servings : 4

Difficulty Level : Average

Ingredients:

- 2 cups cauliflower florets
- 2 cups broccoli florets
- 1 (15-ounce / 425-g) can chickpeas
- 1 cup carrot slices (about 1 inch thick)
- 2 to 3 tablespoons extra-virgin olive oil, divided
- Salt and black pepper, to taste
- Nonstick cooking spray
- 2 cups cooked brown rice
- 3 tablespoons sesame seeds
- <u>Dressing:</u>
- 3 to 4 tablespoons tahini
- 2 tablespoons honey
- 1 lemon, juiced
- 1 garlic clove, minced
- Salt and black pepper, to taste

Directions:

Ready the oven to 400ºF (205ºC). Spritz two baking sheets with nonstick cooking spray.

Spread the cauliflower and broccoli on the first baking sheet and the second with the chickpeas and carrot slices.

Drizzle each sheet with half of the olive oil and sprinkle with salt and pepper. Toss to coat well.

Roast the chickpeas and carrot slices in the preheated oven for 10 minutes, leaving the carrots tender but crisp, and the cauliflower and broccoli for 20 minutes until fork-tender. Stir them once halfway through the cooking time.

Meanwhile, make the dressing: Whisk together the tahini, honey, lemon juice, garlic, salt, and pepper in a small bowl.

Divide the cooked brown rice among four bowls. Top each bowl evenly with roasted vegetables and dressing. Sprinkle the sesame seeds on top for garnish before serving.

Nutrition (for 100g): 453 Calories 17.8g Fat 11.2g Carbohydrates 12.1g Protein 793mg Sodium

Cauliflower Hash with Carrots

Preparation Time : 10 minutes

Cooking Time : 10 minutes

Servings : 4

Difficulty Level : Easy

Ingredients:

- 3 tablespoons extra-virgin olive oil
- 1 large onion, chopped
- 1 tablespoon minced garlic
- 2 cups diced carrots
- 4 cups cauliflower florets
- ½ teaspoon ground cumin
- 1 teaspoon salt

Directions:

Cook the olive oil over medium heat. Mix in the onion and garlic and sauté for 1 minute. Stir in the carrots and stir-fry for 3 minutes. Add the cauliflower florets, cumin, and salt and toss to combine.

Cover and cook for 3 minutes until lightly browned. Stir well and cook, uncovered, for 3 to 4 minutes, until softened. Remove from the heat and serve warm.

Nutrition (for 100g): 158 Calories 10.8g Fat 5.1g Carbohydrates 3.1g Protein 813mg Sodium

Garlicky Zucchini Cubes with Mint

Preparation Time : 5 minutes

Cooking Time : 10 minutes

Servings : 4

Difficulty Level : Easy

Ingredients:

- 3 large green zucchinis
- 3 tablespoons extra-virgin olive oil
- 1 large onion, chopped
- 3 cloves garlic, minced
- 1 teaspoon salt
- 1 teaspoon dried mint

Directions:

Cook the olive oil in a large skillet over medium heat.

Mix in the onion and garlic and sauté for 3 minutes, stirring constantly, or until softened.

Stir in the zucchini cubes and salt and cook for 5 minutes, or until the zucchini is browned and tender.

Add the mint to the skillet and toss to combine, then continue cooking for 2 minutes. Serve warm.

Nutrition (for 100g): 146 Calories 10.6g Fat 3g Carbohydrates 4.2g Protein 789mg Sodium

Zucchini and Artichokes Bowl with Faro

Preparation Time : 15 minutes

Cooking Time : 10 minutes

Servings : 6

Difficulty Level : Easy

Ingredients:

- 1/3 cup extra-virgin olive oil
- 1/3 cup chopped red onions
- ½ cup chopped red bell pepper
- 2 garlic cloves, minced
- 1 cup zucchini, cut into ½-inch-thick slices
- ½ cup coarsely chopped artichokes
- ½ cup canned chickpeas, drained and rinsed
- 3 cups cooked faro
- Salt and black pepper, to taste
- ½ cup crumbled feta cheese, for serving (optional)
- ¼ cup sliced olives, for serving (optional)
- 2 tablespoons fresh basil, chiffonade, for serving (optional)
- 3 tablespoons balsamic vinegar, for serving (optional)

Directions:

Heat up the olive oil in a large skillet over medium heat until it shimmers. Mix the onions, bell pepper, and garlic and sauté for 5 minutes, stirring occasionally, until softened.

Stir in the zucchini slices, artichokes, and chickpeas and sauté for about 5 minutes until slightly tender. Add the cooked faro and toss to combine until heated through. Sprinkle the salt and pepper to season.

Divide the mixture into bowls. Top each bowl evenly with feta cheese, olive slices, and basil and sprinkle with the balsamic vinegar, if desired.

Nutrition (for 100g): 366 Calories 19.9g Fat 9g Carbohydrates 9.3g Protein 819mg Sodium

5-Ingredient Zucchini Fritters

Preparation Time : 15 minutes

Cooking Time : 5 minutes

Servings : 14

Difficulty Level : Average

Ingredients:

- 4 cups grated zucchini
- Salt, to taste
- 2 large eggs, slightly beaten
- 1/3 cup sliced scallions
- 2/3 all-purpose flour
- 1/8 teaspoon black pepper
- 2 tablespoons olive oil

Directions:

Situate the grated zucchini in a colander and lightly season with salt. Set aside to rest for 10 minutes. Grip as much liquid from the grated zucchini as possible.

Pour the grated zucchini into a bowl. Fold in the beaten eggs, scallions, flour, salt, and pepper and stir until everything is well combined.

Heat up the olive oil in a large skillet over medium heat until hot.

Drop 3 tablespoons mounds of the zucchini mixture onto the hot skillet to make each fritter, pin them lightly into rounds and spacing them about 2 inches apart.

Cook for 2 to 3 minutes. Flip the zucchini fritters and cook for 2 minutes more, or until they are golden brown and cooked through.

Remove from the heat to a plate lined with paper towels. Repeat with the remaining zucchini mixture. Serve hot.

Nutrition (for 100g): 113 Calories 6.1g Fat 9g Carbohydrates 4g Protein 793mg Sodium